Utilize este código QR para se cadastrar de forma mais rápida:

Ou, se preferir, entre em:

www.richmond.com.br/ac/livroportal

e siga as instruções para ter acesso aos conteúdos exclusivos do

Portal e Livro Digital

CÓDIGO DE ACESSO:

A 00049 PEACE2E 4 19605

Faça apenas um cadastro. Ele será válido para:

Students for
PEACE

Eduardo Amos
Renata Condi

4

Student's Book & Workbook

Richmond

Richmond

Direção editorial: Sandra Possas

Edição executiva de inglês: Izaura Valverde
Edição executiva de produção e multimídia: Adriana Pedro de Almeida

Coordenação de arte: Raquel Buim
Coordenação de revisão: Rafael Spigel

Edição de texto: Bruna Marini, Ludmila De Nardi, Nathália Horvath, Wilson Chequi
Assistência editorial: Angela Cristina Costa Neves, Cíntia Afarelli Pereira, Leila Scatena
Elaboração de conteúdo: Ana Paula Reis, Beatriz Nosé, Christiane Araújo, Cristina Mayer, Doris Soares
Preparação de originais: Helaine Albuquerque, Roberta Moratto Risther
Revisão: Carolina Waideman, Flora Manzione, Gabriele Martin Cândido, Gislaine Caprioli Costa, Kandy Saraiva, Katia Gouveia Vitale, Márcio Martins, Vivian Cristina de Souza

Projeto gráfico: Carol Duran
Edição de arte: Fabiane Eugenio
Diagramação: APIS design
Capa: Carol Duran
Criações: Anderson Sunakozawa, Camila Ranelli, Fabiane Eugenio, Manuel Miramontes, Mateus Banti

Website: Daniela Carrete, Frodo Almeida (*design*)
Social Media: Ana Paula Campos, Priscila Oliveira Vieira (edição de conteúdo); Eloah Cristina (analista de projetos); Altair Sampaio, Frodo Almeida (*design*)
Digital Hub: Ana Paula Campos, Priscila Oliveira Vieira (edição de conteúdo); Eloah Cristina (analista de projetos); Daniela Carrete (*design*)
PEACE Builders: Ana Paula Campos (edição de conteúdo); Daniela Carrete (*design*)
Digital Academy: Gabrielle Navarro, Thaís Teixeira Tardivo (edição de conteúdo); Daniel Favalli (coordenação de produção); Angela Urbinatti, Mônica M. Oldrine (*design*)
Novo Portal Educacional Richmond: Sheila Rizzi (edição)
Livro Digital Interativo: Gabrielle Navarro, Thaís Teixeira Tardivo (edição de conteúdo); Daniel Favalli (coordenação de produção); Angela Urbinatti (*design*)
Iconografia: Marcia Sato, Sara Alencar
Coordenação de *bureau*: Rubens M. Rodrigues
Tratamento de imagens: Fernando Bertolo, Joel Aparecido, Luiz Carlos Costa, Marina M. Buzzinaro
Pré-impressão: Alexandre Petreca, Everton L. de Oliveira, Márcio H. Kamoto, Vitória Sousa
Áudio: Maximal Studio

Todos os *sites* mencionados nesta obra foram reproduzidos apenas para fins didáticos. A Richmond não tem controle sobre seu conteúdo, o qual foi cuidadosamente verificado antes de sua utilização.
Websites mentioned in this material were quoted for didactic purposes only. Richmond has no control over their content and urges care when using them.

Embora todas as medidas tenham sido tomadas para identificar e contatar os detentores de direitos autorais sobre os materiais reproduzidos nesta obra, isso nem sempre foi possível. A editora estará pronta a retificar quaisquer erros dessa natureza assim que notificada.
Every effort has been made to trace the copyright holders, but if any omission can be rectified, the publishers will be pleased to make the necessary arrangements.

Impressão e acabamento: Coan Indústria Gráfica Ltda.
Lote: 284784 / 284785

Dados Internacionais de Catalogação na Publicação (CIP)
(Câmara Brasileira do Livro, SP, Brasil)

Amos, Eduardo
  Students for peace / Eduardo Amos, Renata Condi. -
- 2. ed. -- São Paulo : Moderna, 2019. -- (Students
for peace)

  Obra em 4 v. do 6º ao 9º ano.

  1. Inglês (Ensino fundamental) I. Condi, Renata.
II. Título. III. Série.

19-26387   CDD-372.652

Índices para catálogo sistemático:
  1. Inglês : Ensino fundamental   372.652
Maria Paula C. Riyuzo - Bibliotecária - CRB-8/7639

ISBN 978-85-16-12054-2 (LA)
ISBN 978-85-16-12055-9 (LP)

Reprodução proibida. Art. 184 do Código Penal e Lei 9.610 de 19 de fevereiro de 1998.
Todos os direitos reservados.

Richmond
EDITORA MODERNA LTDA.
Rua Padre Adelino, 758 – Belenzinho
São Paulo – SP – Brasil – CEP 03303-904
www.richmond.com.br
2019

Impresso no Brasil

Créditos das fotos: Capa: RadomanDurkovic/iStockphoto; p. 7: Kritchanut/iStockphoto; p. 8: SolStock/iStockphoto, Catalin Petolea/Shutterstock; carstenbrandt/iStockphoto; p. 9: Gligatron/iStockphoto; avid_creative/iStockphoto; p. 10: U.S. Department of Labor; p. 13: CreativaImages/iStockphoto; p. 15: StatCrunch; U.S. DEPARTMENT OF LABOR; Commonwealth of Australia, Department of the Prime Minister and Cabinet, Closing the Gap Prime Minister's Report 2018; p. 16: Reprodução; p. 17: Bulgac/iStockphoto; imaginima/iStockphoto; p. 20: David-Prado/iStockphoto, Suwin/Shutterstock; miriamdoerr/iStockphoto; p. 21: vgajic/iStockphoto; Sjoerd van der Wal/iStockphoto; Mukesh Kumar Jwala/Shutterstock; ohnnyGreig/iStockphoto; p. 27: © Randy Glasbergen; p. 28: © Cartoonstock; © Randy Glasbergen; p. 32: Sustainable Development/United Nations; PeskyMonkey/iStockphoto; p. 33: © Witness Project International; p. 34: kate_sept2004/iStockphoto; sadikgulec/iStockphoto; p. 35: South_agency/iStockphoto; Delfim Martins/Pulsar Imagens; Peter Marshall/Alamy/Fotoarena; p. 36: Susana Vera/Reuters/Fotoarena; p. 38: © 2018 King Features Syndicate/Ipress; p. 39: Brian Cane/Washington Post; p. 40: AntonioGuillem/iStockphoto; itsajoop/iStockphoto; designer491/Shutterstock; Global_Pics/iStockphoto, Alphotographic/iStockphoto; Alex Segre/Alamy/Fotoarena; FredFroese/iStockphoto; Chico Ferreira/Pulsar Imagens; p. 46: kanvag/iStockphoto; lucentius/iStockphoto; Miljan Živković/iStockphoto; p. 47: monkeybusinessimages/iStockphoto; LordRunar/iStockphoto; p. 48: WHO/UNICEF JMP; p. 49: Online Master of Engineering Management/Ohio University; p. 53: David Parsons/iStockphoto; AndreyPopov/iStockphoto; Drazen Lovric/iStockphoto; vm/iStockphoto; Ekaterina79/iStockphoto; maljalen/iStockphoto; p. 54: NOAA National Ocean Service; p. 56: ipopba/iStockphoto; p. 58: patpitchaya/iStockphoto; Christiane Elany Britto de Araújo; Jonathan C. Katzenellenbogen/Getty Images; p. 59: Lucian Milasan/Shutterstock; p. 60: silkfactory/iStockphoto; Stuart Forster India/Alamy/Fotoarena; p. 61: LiudmylaSupynska/iStockphoto; William Perugini/Shutterstock; p. 62: hadynyah/iStockphoto; p. 64: hadynyah/iStockphoto; p. 68: Piyaset/Shutterstock; rusm/iStockphoto; Dan Howell/Shutterstock; StanislauV/Shutterstock; Alfribeiro/iStockphoto; p. 69: Rawpixel/iStockphoto; bennyb/iStockphoto; p. 72: Boogich/iStockphoto; oneinchpunch/iStockphoto; p. 73: Barbara Kruger/Mary Boone Gallery, Nova York; tzahiV/iStockphoto; Paolo Bona/Shutterstock; p. 74: Pan American Airlines; p. 75: Western Electric; p. 77: neyro2008/iStockphoto; p. 79: jaminwell/iStockphoto; AdrianHancu/iStockphoto, georgederk/iStockphoto; Justin Kase zsixz/Alamy/Fotoarena; 3Dmask/iStockphoto; Alamy/Fotoarena; ArliftAtoz2205/Shutterstock; p. 80: RuslanDashinsky/iStockphoto; AndreyPopov/iStockphoto; Pollyana Ventura/iStockphoto; Neustockimages/iStockphoto; AndreyPopov/iStockphoto; p. 81: xamtiw/iStockphoto; deepblue4you/iStockphoto; Floortje/iStockphoto; IlyaShapovalov/iStockphoto; gyavcin/iStockphoto; Kintarapong/iStockphoto; membio/iStockphoto; Sinan Kocaslan/iStockphoto; Silberkorn/iStockphoto; ZargonDesign/iStockphoto; p. 82: andresr/iStockphoto; p. 84: Gustavo Frazao/Shutterstock; zlikovec/Shutterstock; p. 86: Puttimedh Varasarin/Shutterstock; John Wollwerth/Shutterstock; MediaWorldImages/Alamy/Fotoarena; p. 87: BSIP SA/Alamy/Fotoarena; Chico Ferreira/Pulsar Imagens; p. 88: Charles Moore/Getty Images; Jonathan Bachman/Reuters/Fotoarena; p. 90: Amnesty Internacional; Gold Trail School District #74; p. 94: © 2018 United Nations. Reprinted with the permission of the United Nations; p. 98: Hulton-Deutsch Collection/Corbis/Getty Images; films for freedom; p. 99: Amnesty Internacional; Ron Ellis/Shutterstock; Bogdan Khmelnytskyi/Shutterstock; p. 100: reprodução; p. 102: Martin Puddy/Getty Images; p. 104: FG Trade/iStockphoto; SensorSpot/iStockphoto; mikimad/iStockphoto; p. 106: gradyreese/iStockphoto; p. 110: © 2015 Matt Wuerker/Dist. by Andrews McMeel Syndication; © 2015 Jeff Stahler/Dist. by Andrews McMeel Syndication for UFS; Adam Fagen; p. 111: traveler1116/iStockphoto; p. 115: Tomwang112/iStockphoto; p. 116: seb_ra/iStockphoto; Rawf8/iStockphoto; selinofoto/Shutterstock; p. 118: andresr/iStockphoto; p. 127: CarrieCaptured/iStockphoto; Macrovector/Shutterstock; Django/iStockphoto; p.123: Coleção Particular; KatarzynaBialasiewicz/iStockphoto; zoroasto/iStockphoto; kajakiki/iStockphoto; WAYHOME studio/Shutterstock; p. 125: sefa ozel/iStockphoto; p. 127: ip Archive/Glow Images; p. 142: Ten Speed Press; Ruby Films; Brandstorm Entertainment; p. 143: Penguin Random House; Back Bay Books; Das Kollektiv für audiovisuelle Werke.

Dear student,

This is **Students for PEACE** – a set of materials designed not only to help you learn English, but also to make you think about, discuss and act upon important issues related to your life and your community. **Students for PEACE** is the result of many years of study and research.

When we first sat down to write this series, we felt that we had to go beyond the study of the English language because there was something the world needed desperately – peace. And it still needs it. So we decided to make peace education the core of this series and its goal. The ideas presented in **Students for PEACE** are based on the positive concept of peace as justice, tolerance and respect.

This series will certainly help you learn English, but we hope it will also help you understand and acknowledge human diversity and live with one another in harmony, facing the different challenges of the world around you.

As those famous song lyrics said, "All we are saying is give peace a chance!"

Have a nice year!

Editorial team

Scope & sequence

Welcome Chapter (p. 6) — What world would you like to live in?

	Goals	Explore & Studio	Building blocks & Toolbox	Sync – Listening & Sync – Speaking
1 The world of work (p. 8)	• Acknowledge the value of different occupations and the role of education in choosing them. • Present data from a survey orally. • Reflect on the issue of equal opportunities for men and women in the world of work. • Review the use of the future with "will" and the future with "going to". • Understand a recording about remote work and flexible schedule. • Understand and produce graphs to show data.	• Graph	• Types of graphs • "Will" x "going to" (review)	• Remote jobs • Survey report
2 Tech in the world (p. 20)	• Identify collocations and the use of prefixes in technology-related words. • Reflect on the positive and the negative aspects of modern technology in our lives. • Understand and make a chart with data from a survey. • Understand and prepare a mini-lesson based on visuals (charts, graphs, notes etc.). • Understand the use of conditionals to refer to things that are always true (type zero) and things that are likely to happen in the future under given circumstances (type 1).	• Chart	• Technology • Conditional sentences – types zero and 1	• A video lesson on technology • How things work
Peace talk (p. 32)	Promoting gender equality			
3 Citizenship (p. 34)	• Make an oral presentation about different types of governments expressing your opinion about them. • Recognize and use "have to", "must" and "should" to express obligation, (lack of) necessity, prohibition and to make recommendations. • Reflect about citizenship and the characteristics of a good citizen. • Understand an audio about democracy. • Understand and write posts in a debate forum. • Use vocabulary to name the rights and responsibilities of a citizen.	• Forum post	• Rights and responsibilities • Expressing obligation and recommendation ("have to", "must", "should")	• Democracy • Democracy and other types of governments around the world
4 Sustainability (p. 46)	• Create an oral testimonial about initiatives related to sustainability. • Learn some verbs used to describe environmental impact and how to reduce it. • Reflect on which daily attitudes help protect the planet and which ones may harm it. • Review the use of the modals "should", "have to" and "must" to express recommendation, necessity or obligation. • Understand and create infographics about the environment and sustainability. • Understand and use the modals "may", "might" and "will" to express probability. • Understand oral testimonials.	• Infographic	• Verbs to describe environmental impact and how to reduce it • Modals of probability ("may", "might", "will")	• Testimonials about helping the environment • Testimonial
Peace talk (p. 58)	We are born free and equal			

	Goals	Explore & Studio	Building blocks & Toolbox	Sync – Listening & Sync – Speaking
5 **Global and local** (p. 60)	• Identify the use of the present perfect to express actions that started in the past and extend into the present. • Reflect on the interconnection between local and global situations, especially regarding languages, and on the positive and negative aspects of globalization, with a focus on cultural aspects. • Understand a monologue defending an opinion. • Understand and use expressions to present points of view, arguments and counterarguments. • Understand and write an opinion article.	• Opinion article	• Expressing points of view, arguments and counterarguments • Present perfect with "for" and "since"	• Global challenges • A debate
6 **Consumer society** (p. 72)	• Create a radio commercial. • Learn about different methods to advertise products and services. • Learn about different methods to pay for a product or service. • Reflect on consumerism and the advertising discourse. • Understand an audio about the history of consumerism. • Understand and produce an advertisement. • Understand and use the present perfect with "ever", "already", "yet" and "never".	• Advertisement	• Types of advertising and money vocabulary • Present perfect with "ever", "already", "yet" and "never"	• The history of consumerism • Radio commercial
Peace talk (p. 84)	Happiness comes from within			
7 **Fighting for our rights** (p. 86)	• Create an awareness campaign about people's rights. • Discuss an issue related to human rights, presenting arguments and considering different points of view. • Review and use the present simple, past simple and present perfect. • Understand an interview about racism. • Understand and use connectors (linking words). • Understand the characteristics of a photojournalism article. • Understand the characteristics of an awareness campaign.	• Photojournalism article • Campaign on people's rights	• Connectors (linking words) • Present simple x past simple x present perfect	• Give nothing to racism • Discussing human rights
8 **Freedom of speech** (p. 98)	• Express opinions, arguments and counterarguments in a deliberative conversation. • Identify new writing forms in digital messages. • Reflect on freedom of speech and the right to express ideas and opinions in face-to-face and virtual environments, especially on social media. • Understand and write an editorial. • Understand the use of conditionals type 2 to refer to hypothetical situations. • Understand viewpoints in a deliberative conversation.	• Editorial	• Internet language • Conditional sentences – type 2	• Expressing opinions and reaching a consensus • A deliberative conversation
Peace talk (p. 110)	Agree to disagree			

Self-assessment 112
Workbook 113
Irregular verbs list 129
Language reference 130
Interdisciplinary project 134
Transcripts 136
Glossary 140
Learning more 142
Track list 144
References 144

Welcome to Students for PEACE!

What world would you like to live in?

1 Read the questions and write down your answers.

a What do you want your legacy to be?

b Think of a good thing from the past. How did it change who you are now?

g What do you like most about the world you live in?

c What will be different in the next 10 years? What will be your role in that?

f How can you make a difference to the world you live in?

e How do you want people to see you?

d How can social media make a difference to our world?

a _____
b _____
c _____
d _____
e _____
f _____
g _____

2 Get into groups. Then share your answers with your classmates. What do you have in common?

3 Work with your group and write sentences that summarize your ideas.

4 Create posters with the sentences you wrote in activity 3. Remember to include drawings or pictures. If necessary, use the poster below as a visual reference for your own work.

J.K. Rowling

5 Present the world you would like to live in using the posters. Follow the instructions.

- Study your posters before the presentation.
- Practice what you are going to say.
- Make eye contact with the audience and encourage them to make comments and questions.

1 The world of work

Goals

- Acknowledge the value of different occupations and the role of education in choosing them.
- Present data from a survey orally.
- Reflect on the issue of equal opportunities for men and women in the world of work.
- Review the use of the future with "will" and the future with "going to".
- Understand a recording about remote work and flexible schedule.
- Understand and produce graphs to show data.

Spark

1 What occupations are represented in the pictures? Check.

- [ ] agricultural worker
- [ ] civil engineer
- [ ] dentist
- [ ] lawyer
- [ ] pilot
- [ ] sanitation worker
- [ ] teacher
- [ ] web designer

2 In your opinion, what is the importance of each of these professionals for our society? What would happen if these occupations didn't exist?

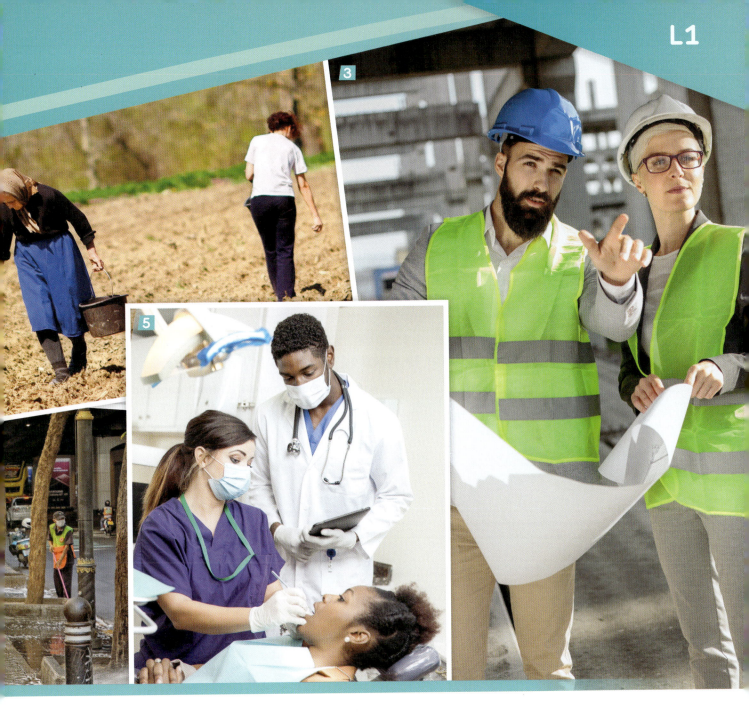

 Look at the pictures again and answer the questions.

a Are all these occupations common in your city/community? How often do you see these professionals?

b Consider the characteristics of each occupation in the pictures. In your opinion, what situations may lead these professionals to feel some of the emotions in the box? Explain.

> anger   disappointment   dislike
> frustration   irritation   nervousness

Listen to:
Digital gender equality

L1

Explore Graph

Pre-reading

1 Discuss these questions with your classmates.

a Do you know what career you want to follow? Explain.

b In your opinion, what careers are more attractive to young people? Why?

2 Take a look at the text and answer the questions.

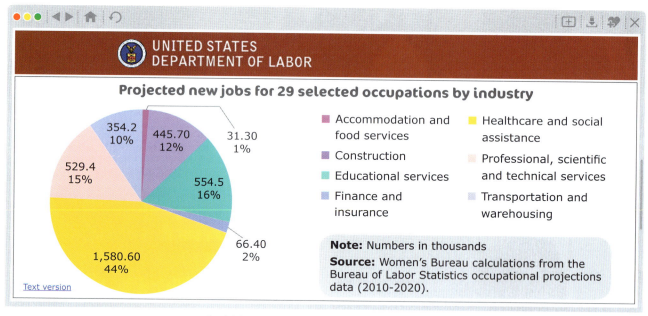

Available at <https://www.dol.gov/wb/stats/idoccupations.htm>. Accessed on March 28, 2019.

a What kind of text is this? Check.

☐ A pie chart.   ☐ A recipe.   ☐ An article.

b What is the purpose of this kind of text?

_____

c Where was this text taken from? Where else can this kind of text be found?

_____

d Which of these options best describes the format of the text?

☐ It's a bar graph (vertical or horizontal bars).   ☐ It's a pie chart (circular chart).

e Which of these characteristics can apply to the text?

☐ A key is added to explain the data.

☐ Contrasting colors are used to represent different data.

☐ Footnotes are used to give background information.

☐ The presentation of the information is visually attractive.

☐ More emphasis is put on the nonverbal elements.

Reading

3 Now read the text in activity 2 and write if the statements are *T* (true) or *F* (false).

a ☐ The numbers on the pie chart divisions/slices are written in a concise/short way.

b ☐ The website doesn't have an alternative description of the information presented by this graph.

c ☐ The graph presents data about projected new jobs for 29 selected occupations for the period of a decade in the United States.

4 The following text is the source of the data presented in the pie chart in activity 2. Read the questions and match them to their answers.

a What do you call this type of text arrangement?

b How would you compare the information provided in this text to the information provided in the pie chart?

☐ The text is more complex and detailed than the pie chart.

☐ It's a chart.

SELECTED IN-DEMAND OCCUPATIONS, 2010-2020 PROJECTIONS

Occupation Name	Projected Growth Number (new jobs in thousands) 2010-2020	Typical Education Level for Entry
Accountants and auditors	190.7	Bachelor's
Brickmasons and blockmasons	41.8	High School
Cargo and freight agents	24.1	High School
Carpenters	196	High School
Cement masons and concrete finishers	50.1	High School
Cost estimators	67.5	Bachelor's
Database administrators	33.9	Bachelor's
Dental hygienists	68.5	Associate's
Elementary school teachers, except special ed	248.8	Bachelor's
Healthcare social workers	51.2	Bachelor's
Heating, air conditioning and refrigeration mechanics and installers	90.3	Postsecondary
Heavy and tractor-trailer truck drivers	330.1	High School
Interpreters and translators	24.6	Bachelor's
Licensed practical and vocational nurses	168.5	Postsecondary
Market research analysts and marketing specialists	116.6	Bachelor's
Medical scientists, except epidemiologists	36.4	Doctoral or Professional
Meeting, convention and event planners	31.3	Bachelor's
Mental health and substance abuse social workers	39.5	Bachelor's
Mental health counselors	43.6	Master's
Occupational therapists	36.4	Master's
Personal financial advisors	66.4	Bachelor's
Physical therapists	77.4	Master's
Physical therapists assistants	30.8	Associate's
Physician assistants	24.7	Master's
Physicians and surgeons	168.3	Doctoral or Professional
Postsecondary teachers	305.7	Doctoral or Professional
Registered nurses	711.9	Associate's
Sales representatives, wholesale and manufacturing	223.4	High School
Software developers, systems software	127.2	Bachelor's

Available at <https://www.dol.gov/wb/stats/occupations.htm>. Accessed on March 29, 2019.

L1

5 Read some of the occupations from the text in activity 4 and write the corresponding industries according to the pie chart in activity 2.

INDUSTRY	OCCUPATIONS
Finance and insurance	○ personal financial advisors
	○ database administrators
	○ heating, air conditioning and refrigeration mechanics and installers
	○ cargo and freight agents
	○ heavy and tractor-trailer truck drivers
	○ meeting, convention and event planners
	○ registered nurses
	○ physicians and surgeons
	○ brickmasons and blockmasons
	○ elementary school teachers, except special ed
	○ postsecondary teachers

Post-reading

6 Answer the questions. Then talk to a partner.

a In your opinion, what will be the most in-demand and fast-growing jobs in Brazil in the next decade? Explain.

_____

b Is there any area or occupation mentioned in the two texts presented in this section that seems interesting to you? If so, which one?

_____

c Most of the occupations with the highest percentage increase in the healthcare and social assistance industry require a Master's degree, according to the chart in activity 4. How can this information be helpful to the new generation of workers? Check the best option.

☐ It helps this generation understand the importance of formal education when they think about their future occupation.

☐ It helps this generation understand that they will face competition in the future.

L2

Toolbox "Will" x "going to" (review)

1 Look at the picture. What does it show? After presenting your ideas, discuss the questions with a partner.

a Do you believe that it is time for you to think about your future career? Why?

_____

b Do you think that the career choices you make now might change in the upcoming years? How?

_____

c In your opinion, what can help someone get a job more easily? Choose the appropriate options.

- [ ] Sending out less than five applications per week.
- [ ] Sending out a large number of applications per week.
- [ ] Writing a traditional *résumé* (*curriculum vitae*).
- [ ] Writing a customized *résumé* (*curriculum vitae*).

> **Language clue**
>
> *Résumé* is a French word. It's another term for *curriculum vitae* (*CV*).

2 Read the text and check if your answers in item "c" from activity **1** reflect the author's opinions.

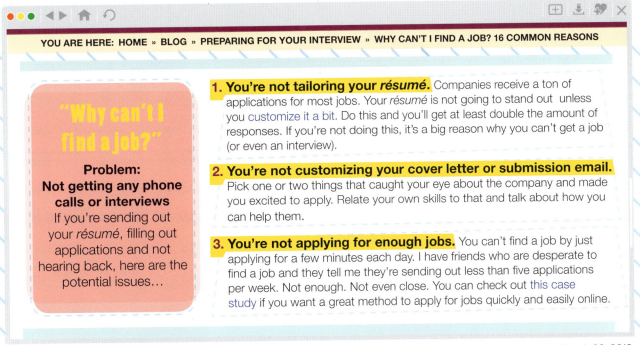

YOU ARE HERE: HOME » BLOG » PREPARING FOR YOUR INTERVIEW » WHY CAN'T I FIND A JOB? 16 COMMON REASONS

"Why can't I find a job?"

Problem: Not getting any phone calls or interviews

If you're sending out your *résumé*, filling out applications and not hearing back, here are the potential issues…

1. You're not tailoring your *résumé*. Companies receive a ton of applications for most jobs. Your *résumé* is not going to stand out unless you customize it a bit. Do this and you'll get at least double the amount of responses. If you're not doing this, it's a big reason why you can't get a job (or even an interview).

2. You're not customizing your cover letter or submission email. Pick one or two things that caught your eye about the company and made you excited to apply. Relate your own skills to that and talk about how you can help them.

3. You're not applying for enough jobs. You can't find a job by just applying for a few minutes each day. I have friends who are desperate to find a job and they tell me they're sending out less than five applications per week. Not enough. Not even close. You can check out this case study if you want a great method to apply for jobs quickly and easily online.

Available at <https://careersidekick.com/why-cant-i-find-a-job/>. Accessed on March 29, 2019.

L2

3 Check the appropriate options to complete the sentences about the text.

a The objective of the text is…

☐ to present reasons why someone can't find a job.

☐ to present reasons why someone doesn't succeed at a job interview.

b The words in bold in the sentence "Your *résumé* **is not going to stand out** unless you customize it a bit." suggest that…

☐ your *résumé* is certainly not going to stand out unless you customize it.

☐ your *résumé* might not stand out unless you customize it.

c The words in bold in the sentence "Do this and **you'll get** at least double the amount of responses." express…

☐ a future probability based on an opinion.   ☐ a plan for the future.

4 Study the quoted sentences in items "b" and "c" from activity 3 and answer the questions.

a Do the words in bold in item "c" refer to an affirmative or to a negative sentence?

_____

b Do the words in bold in item "b" refer to an affirmative or to a negative sentence?

_____

c How do you turn the affirmative form you have identified into the negative form?

_____

d How do you turn the negative form you have identified into the affirmative form?

_____

5 Now complete these rules based on your observations in the previous activities.

a The structure to express a prediction about the future based on evidence or a plan for the future is: verb _____ + _____ + main verb in the infinitive (affirmative form); verb _____ + _____ + _____ + main verb in the infinitive (negative form).

b The structure to express a prediction about the future based on an opinion is: auxiliary _____ + main verb in the infinitive (affirmative form); auxiliary _____ + _____ + main verb in the infinitive (negative form).

6 Write sentences about your future career. What are your plans? What do you think will happen? Use these sentence starters.

| I'm going to… | I think I'll… | I'm not going to… | I probably won't… |

_____

_____

Building blocks Types of graphs

1 Take a look at the graphs 1-4 and answer the questions.

a Which of these types of graph have you seen earlier in this chapter? What do you call it?
_____

b Besides the hyperlinks, two graphs mention their sources. What are they?
_____

c Which graphs mention the years related to the data?
_____

Graph 1

Result 1: Pie Chart of nursing job satisfaction

Job satisfaction
- neutral, 17, 17%
- satisfied, 51, 51%
- unsatisfied, 6, 6%
- very satisfied, 26, 26%

It can be seen that slightly over half of the nurses surveyed are satisfied with their job, while over a quarter, 26%, are very satisfied, an even smaller percent, 17%, are neutral. Only a small percentage, 6%, is unsatisfied with their job.

Available at <https://www.statcrunch.com/5.0/viewreport.php?reportid=25292>. Accessed on March 29, 2019.

Graph 2

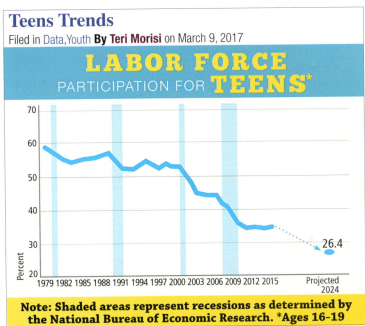

Teens Trends
Filed in Data, Youth **By Teri Morisi** on March 9, 2017

LABOR FORCE PARTICIPATION FOR TEENS*

26.4 Projected 2024

Note: Shaded areas represent recessions as determined by the National Bureau of Economic Research. *Ages 16-19

Available at <https://blog.dol.gov/2017/03/09/teens-trends>. Accessed on March 29, 2019.

Graph 3

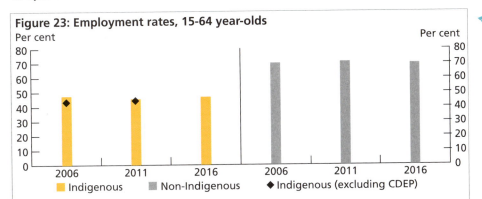

Figure 23: Employment rates, 15-64 year-olds

■ Indigenous   ■ Non-Indigenous   ♦ Indigenous (excluding CDEP)

Estimate of employment rate by removing CDEP participants from employment data. As the Census only asks Australians in remote areas about their CDEP status, it is likely to overestimate the excluding-CDEP employment rate. The CDEP program did not exist in 2016 so no estimate is shown.
Sources: ABS Census of Population and Housing 2006, 2011 and 2016

Language clue

CDEP (Community Development Employment Projects) are an initiative of the Australian government to guarantee jobs for the indigenous communities in the country.

Available at <https://www.pmc.gov.au/sites/default/files/reports/closing-the-gap-2018/employment.html>. Accessed on April 12, 2019.

Graph 4

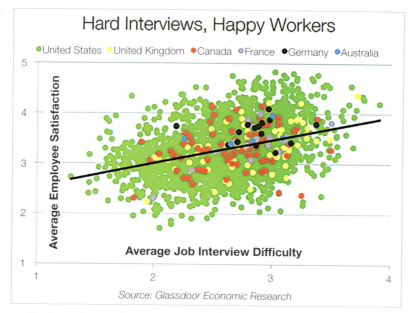

Available at <https://www.glassdoor.com/research/studies/interview-difficulty/>.
Accessed on March 29, 2019.

2 Read the descriptions of the types of graph presented in activity 1. Match each graph to its corresponding description.

Graph 1   Graph 2   Graph 3   Graph 4

a Bar (or column) graphs: these graphs use vertical or horizontal bars to visually show and compare values. The higher or longer the bar, the greater the value.

b Pie graphs (also called "pie charts"): circular graphs that visually represent the size relationship between the parts or percentages and the total amount. The "pie" is divided into sectors (slices), which have different sizes and are often identified with different colors.

c Line graphs (also called "line charts"): lines that help visualize the variation of something over a parameter (usually over time). They can have a single line or a group of lines, depending on the number of variables being showed. They have a horizontal axis, which usually shows the parameter, and a vertical axis, which generally shows a percentage or some other value.

d Scatter plots: graphs of plotted points that display the relationship between two or more sets of data and determine the extent of correlation between them (if any). If there is a correlation, the points appear concentrated near a straight line. If no correlation exists, the points appear randomly scattered.

Going further

There are some other types of graphs besides the ones seen here: **pictograph**, **histogram**, **area chart**, **combo chart**, **radar graph** etc. Search for information about them and share the results with the class.

Sync Listening: Remote jobs

Pre-listening

1 Look at the pictures. What do they show? Then talk to a partner.

a If you could choose, in which of these places would you prefer to work? Why?

b Do you think it is possible to work for a company from home? Answer with examples.

Listening

2 🎧 2 Listen to the introduction of an oral text about new ways of working. Complete the excerpt with the missing verbs.

"The world of work is _____. It's no longer a place where we _____ or where we _____ from. Work is wherever we _____ it to be."

3 🎧 3 Now listen to the whole audio and check the appropriate options.

a Mobile technology is growing by…

☐ 15% every year. ☐ 50% every year. ☐ 60% every year.

b 70% of employees prefer to work…

☐ remotely. ☐ in the company. ☐ anywhere.

c People are…

☐ still governed by the nine-to-five job. ☐ no longer governed by the nine-to-five job.

d Mobile workers are…

☐ more connected, more motivated, but less productive.
☐ more connected, more motivated and more productive.

Post-listening

4 Discuss the questions with your classmates.

a Based on the audio, does the possibility of working more flexibly bring positive or negative changes?

b Have you ever participated in a remote class? If so, how was it? If not, would you like to have this experience? Why?

L3

Sync Speaking: **Survey report**

Pre-speaking

1 In your opinion, what professional areas are the people in your class most interested in?

2 Carry out a survey to find out what professional areas interest the students in your class the most. Follow the instructions.

   a Work in groups. Prepare the questions you will ask your classmates.

   b Ask the students in another group about their favorite professional area.

   c Here are some professional areas you may consider for this survey.

> Arts, Design and Performance   Banking and Finance   Law
> CHARITY AND VOLUNTARY WORK   Healthcare   CONSULTING AND MANAGEMENT
> EDUCATION   ENGINEERING AND MANUFACTURING   SALES AND MARKETING
> Communication and Media   INFORMATION TECHNOLOGY   SPORT
> Environment and Agriculture   SCIENCE

3 Organize the data you have collected and create a pie chart. Consider the percentage of students that found each professional area the most appealing.

4 Use the data your group has collected to plan an oral presentation for your classmates. The pie chart you have created and the "Useful language" box might help you.

> **Useful language**
> - The purpose/aim of this report is to present the results of the survey we carried out with…
> - The minority/majority of students said that…
> - …% of the students we surveyed indicated that…
> - The results suggest/imply that…
> - The conclusion that we can draw from this survey is that…

Speaking

5 Present the results of the survey to the whole class.

Post-speaking

6 Write *E* (easy) or *D* (difficult) according to your opinion about your work.

   a ☐ Carrying out the survey.

   b ☐ Organizing the collected data to create a pie chart.

   c ☐ Reporting the results to your classmates.

   d ☐ Using the pie chart as a support during the presentation.

> **What:** a bar graph
> **To whom:** other students, people in general
> **Media:** paper; digital
> **Objective:** display the data from a research

1. Review the characteristics of bar graphs. What are they? How are they different from pie charts?

2. Retrieve the data you collected for the oral presentation in the "Sync – Speaking" section (professional areas that appeal the most to the students in your class) to create a bar graph.

3. Create a first draft of your bar graph. Make sure you include some of the typical elements of a graph: title, subtitle, footnotes, key, data labels.

4. Share your draft with your classmates. Give and receive feedback.

5. Revise your text based on the feedback received. Decide if it would be necessary to ask for some more feedback.

6. Write the final version of your bar graph. This can be done on paper or, in case computers are available, you can also create a digital version.

7. Share your bar graph with the whole class. You can also display it on the school bulletin board so that everybody can have access to the results of the survey you carried out.

8. Publish your work on the **Students for PEACE Social Media** <www.studentsforpeace.com.br>, using the tag **graph** or others chosen by the students.

2 Tech in the world

An agricultural _____ on a farm

_____ at an airport

A medical assistance _____ in a hospital

Goals

- Identify collocations and the use of prefixes in technology-related words.
- Reflect on the positive and the negative aspects of modern technology in our lives.
- Understand and make a chart with data from a survey.
- Understand and prepare a mini-lesson based on visuals (charts, graphs, notes etc.).
- Understand the use of conditionals to refer to things that are always true (type zero) and things that are likely to happen in the future under given circumstances (type 1).

Spark

 Look at the pictures and use the words from the box to complete their captions.

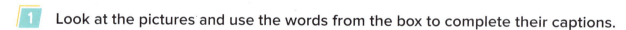

drone   infotainment system   laptop   prosthetic leg   robot
self-check-in kiosks   virtual-reality headset

2 Discuss the questions with your classmates.

a What connections can you make between the pictures and the theme of this chapter?

b Have you ever used/seen any of the technologies in the pictures? Which one/s?

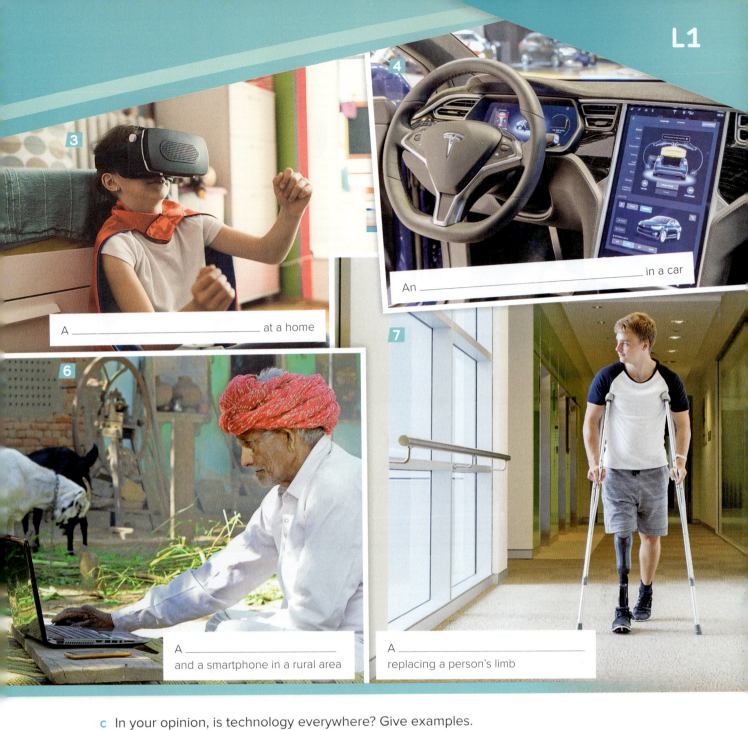

A _____ at a home

An _____ in a car

A _____ and a smartphone in a rural area

A _____ replacing a person's limb

c In your opinion, is technology everywhere? Give examples.

_____

_____

3 Check the statements you agree with and talk to a partner.

a Will robots be similar to humans one day?

☐ That's impossible. Machines will never be able to have feelings.

☐ Maybe. Some robots now can even write texts/music and recognize emotions.

b Is technology making people unsociable and insensitive?

☐ Yes. People don't go out anymore. They talk and have fun via technology.

☐ No. We are now closer to our friends and family with the help of technology.

Pre-reading

1 Talk to a partner about these questions.

   a Do you use social media apps and sites? If so, which ones?

   b How often do you use them?

   c What's your favorite social media type? Explain.

2 What's your opinion about social media in general? Check the best option and collect your classmates' answers.

☐ It's my favorite online activity! I'm always posting personal content (pictures, texts, videos etc.), talking to my friends and checking their storylines and posts.

☐ I like to be on social media, but I don't post much personal content.

☐ I don't care about social media. I think it's a waste of time.

Reading

3 Look at this chart with data from a survey on social media carried out with teens. Match the sentences to the sections in the chart. Follow the example.

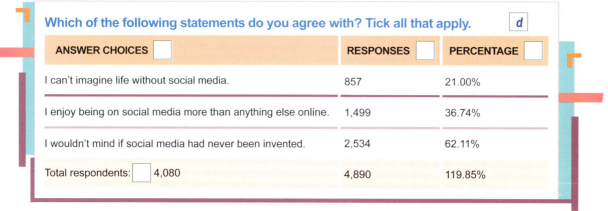

Adapted from <https://www.hmc.org.uk/wp-content/uploads/2017/10/Tech-Control-Survey.pdf>. Accessed on April 1, 2019.

   a The options the respondents could choose from.

   b The percentage of answers in each option.

   c The number of people who chose each option.

   d ~~Instructions to the respondents.~~

   e The number of people who answered the survey.

4 Read the chart again and circle the appropriate options to complete this statement.

The number of respondents is **equal to**/**different from** the number of responses because respondents **could**/**could not** choose more than one option.

22

5 Read the headline and the lead of this news article. Check the appropriate options.

Growing social media backlash among young people, survey shows

Almost two-thirds of pupils say they would not care if the technology did not exist and talk of negative impact on wellbeing

The Guardian, London, October 5, 2017.

a This text will present…

- [ ] facts based on a survey about social media.
- [ ] the journalist's opinion about social media.

b This article will probably confirm that…

- [ ] young people are more interested in social media.
- [ ] young people are less interested in social media.

c The word "backlash" probably refers to…

- [ ] a positive reaction by a large number of people.
- [ ] a negative reaction by a large number of people.

6 Now read this extract from the article and confirm your answers to activity 5.

Almost two-thirds of schoolchildren would not mind if social media had never been invented, a survey has indicated.

The study provides evidence that young people are disillusioned with the negative aspects of the technology, such as online abuse and fake news.

As well as the 63% who would not care if it did not exist, most students (71%) said they had taken temporary digital detoxes to escape social media. (I) One of the reasons is that social media didn't make over 50% of them feel more confident about how they look or how interesting their life is. (II)

The survey of about 5,000 students at independent and state schools in England was commissioned by Digital Awareness UK and the Headmasters' and Headmistresses' Conference (HMC) and it was carried out in September.

Adapted from *The Guardian*, London, October 5, 2017.

L1

7 Compare and match sentences I and II from the article in activity 6 with these charts displaying data from the survey.

a ☐

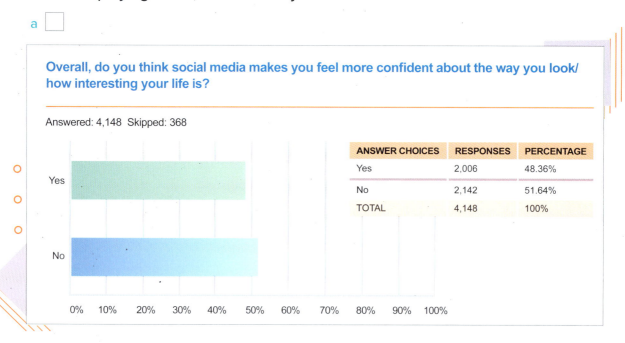

b ☐

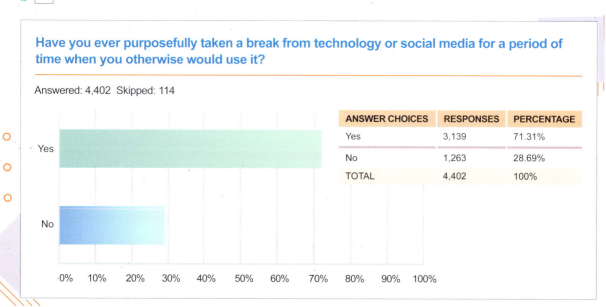

Excerpts adapted from <https://www.hmc.org.uk/wp-content/uploads/2017/10/Tech-Control-Survey.pdf>. Accessed on April 1, 2019.

Post-reading

8 Discuss these questions with your classmates.

a What is your opinion about the survey? Is there anything that surprised you?

b How similar is the data you collected in activity 2 to the data from the article?

c Did the charts help you understand the data presented in the article?

L2

Toolbox: Conditional sentences – types zero and 1

1 Read these comments on technology. Tell a partner if you agree or disagree with each of them. Use the phrases in the boxes below.

a "Social media is something amazing. But if online abuse and fake news take control of this media, we all lose."

Adapted from *The Guardian*, London, October 5, 2017.

b "Unless we are more careful, technology will destroy us."

Adapted from <http://markanderson.bangordailynews.com/2016/02/07/opinion/unless-we-are-more-careful-technology-will-doom-us/>. Accessed on April 22, 2019.

c "If there's a word you really want to understand, you just search the internet."

Adapted from <http://www.aginginplace.org/technology-in-our-life-today-and-how-it-has-changed/>. Accessed on April 22, 2019.

d "We will value artists and their creations more, even if a robot can do it better. For example, we will value how long it took a musician to learn to produce such amazing music. It's the human journey that will become important."

Adapted from *The Guardian*, London, October 13, 2016.

Expressing opinion
I agree.   I disagree in part.
I agree in part. I totally disagree.

Asking your partner's opinion
What about you?

Agreeing with your partner
Me too.
Me neither.

---

2 Analyze the highlighted statements from activity 1 and circle the best options.

a There is one/There are two clause/s in each statement.

b The clauses that introduce a condition in each statement are **blue/pink/yellow**.

c The clauses that express what generally happens or is true in each statement are **blue/pink/yellow**.

d The clauses that express what is possible to happen in each statement are **blue/pink/yellow**.

3 Read the statements in activity 1 again and check the appropriate options.

a "If", "unless" and "even if" are conjunctions that introduce…

☐ results.   ☐ conditions.

b In clauses that introduce conditions, the verbs are used in the…

☐ present.   ☐ future.

c In clauses that express what generally happens or is true, the verbs are used in the…

☐ present.   ☐ future.

d In clauses that express what is possible, but not certain, to happen, the verbs are used in the…

☐ present.   ☐ future.

e Clauses that express condition _____ come before or after the main clause.

☐ may   ☐ may not

25

L2

4 Choose the appropriate options in the box to complete this summary about conditional clauses.

> future (with "will" + verb)   present

- To refer to things that are always true or generally happen under certain conditions, we use: "if"/"unless"/"even if" + subject + verb in the _____ and the main clause in the _____.

- To refer to things that are possible or probable to happen under certain conditions, we use: "if"/"unless"/"even if" + subject + verb in the _____ and the main clause in the _____.

5 Complete these sentences with the appropriate form of the verbs in parentheses.

a If I _____ the meaning of a word in English, I _____ an online dictionary. (not know; use)

b If I _____ a link from an unknown number in my messenger app, I _____ it. (receive; not open)

c If I _____ to learn how to use an app, I _____ how-to videos online. (need; watch)

d If I _____ to learn about my favorite singers, I _____ them. (want; google)

6 With a partner, make predictions about the future. Use the ideas in a-c.

> What will happen if we have self-driving cars?

> If we have self-driving cars, people won't have to learn how to drive anymore.

a We have self-driving cars.
_____
_____

b We install green rooftops in our community.
_____
_____

c We use 3-D printing in medicine.
_____
_____

Building blocks Technology

1 Read the cartoon and write *T* (true) or *F* (false).

"My smartphone communicates with my smartwatch and smart TV. I think they're calling me 'stupid' behind my back."

a ☐ The man is at the psychoanalyst.
b ☐ He has a technical problem with his smartphone.
c ☐ He believes his electronic devices think he is not intelligent.

2 Add at least one more word to each item to make collocations related to technology.

a **smart:** (smart)phone,
b **digital:** camera,
c **nano:** (nano)medicine,
d **online:** shopping,
e **virtual:** reality,

3 Match these opposing prefixes used in technology-related words.

a up   ☐ low
b high   ☐ out
c in   ☐ down

L2

4 Complete the cartoons with some of the prefixes from activity 3.

a

b

c

"This restaurant has an app that lets you _____ load parmesan cheese from the cloud!"

d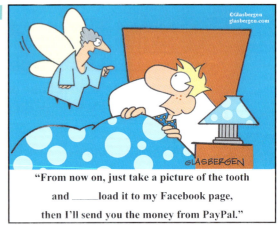

"From now on, just take a picture of the tooth and _____ load it to my Facebook page, then I'll send you the money from PayPal."

5 Match the explanations to the corresponding cartoons in activity 4.

☐ Technology is sometimes too complex and useless.
☐ Sometimes adults know less about technology than teens.
☐ Technology makes it possible for us to do some things virtually.
☐ It's a play on words ("download" and "cloud").

6 Complete the questions using the words from activity 4. Then talk to a partner about the answers.

a What kind of apps do you usually _____?

☐ Dictionaries.   ☐ Games.
☐ Social media.   ☐ Others: _____

b How often do you _____ pictures to your social media?

☐ I always post new pictures.   ☐ I sometimes do it.   ☐ I never do it.

c If scientists invented a device to _____ information into your brain, what would you say?

☐ That's awesome! Give me one, please!
☐ Let's wait and see what happens to other people.
☐ This is very dangerous! I don't want to have it.

L3

Sync Listening: **A video lesson on technology**

Pre-listening

1 Discuss this question with your classmates.

a How often do you use computer technology? Where can you find it?

Listening

2 🎧 4 Listen to a lesson about computers and write *T* (true) or *F* (false).

a ☐ The lesson is about what makes a computer a computer.
b ☐ The speakers don't talk about the history of computers.
c ☐ They explain in details the four tasks computers do.
d ☐ They say that modern computers have something in common with old computers.

3 🎧 5 Now listen to part 2 of the lesson again and use this schema to take notes.

1. Tools help us _____. They help with:
   - _____ work: moving or manipulating _____ like dirt and stone (e.g.: wheelbarrow, tractor trailer).
   - _____ work: manipulating _____ (e.g.: solving equations, tracking stars in the sky).

2. Thinking machines:
   - _____ input
   - Process it
   - Store _____
   - Output _____

   } 4 tasks common to all computers

4 🎧 6 Listen to part 3 of the lesson again and complete this chart with the central ideas about modern computers. Then compare it with a partner.

	OLD COMPUTERS	MODERN COMPUTERS
Materials	Made of wood and metal.	
Functions	Started out as basic calculators (manipulated only numbers).	
Comments	Really large and slow. Size of a room. Took hours to do a basic math problem.	

Post-listening

5 Did the notes you took help you remember what you heard in the audio? Why?

L3

Sync Speaking: How things work

Pre-speaking

1 Discuss these questions with a partner.

  a Name three different types of technology you see around you.

  b Do you know how they work?

2 Let's prepare a mini-lesson about a piece of technology.

  a Get into groups. Choose a piece of technology you are familiar with.

  b Find more information about it (e.g.: its history, how it works, statistics about its use, tips on how to use it, the probability of this technology existing in the future etc.).

  c Prepare your mini-lesson based on the transcript of track 4. If necessary, use the dictionary or ask your teacher/classmates to help with the words you do not know.

  d Prepare slides or posters with graphs, charts, bullet points with keywords etc. to summarize the central points and make your mini-lesson more interesting.

  e Think about the possibility of demonstrating how to use the technology.

  f Decide who is going to present each part of the mini-lesson. Practice your part in front of other group members and listen to their parts as well.

  g Make comments about all parts of the mini-lesson (if they are clear, if the visuals help you understand the topics) and listen to the feedback about your part. Make changes if necessary.

Speaking

3 Now you are going to deliver your mini-lesson.

  a In groups, introduce the topic of your lesson.

  b Present it using the visual support.

  c If possible, demonstrate how to use the piece of technology you chose and answer questions.

Post-speaking

4 Discuss these questions with your classmates.

  a In your opinion, which of the technologies presented has the most interesting history?

  b Do the technologies presented have anything in common? Explain.

  c Would you like to be an inventor or a designer and work with science and technology? Explain.

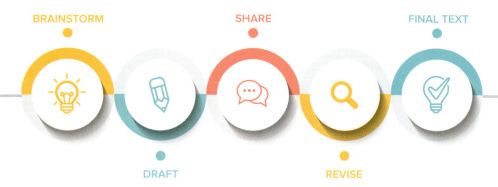

> **What:** a chart and a paragraph
> **To whom:** other students; people in general
> **Media:** digital; paper
> **Objective:** present survey results

1. Work in groups. Choose one of these topics to investigate (or others you may want to): Do old people fear technology? Do my friends need digital detoxing? What technologies do my friends use the most?

2. Prepare questions to ask people in order to collect information about the topic.

3. Interview people.

4. Organize the data you collected in categories (e.g.: age, gender, profession, answers to each question etc.).

5. Revise the characteristics of charts in the "Explore" section.

6. Prepare one or more charts to display the information collected.

7. Write your paragraph: introduce the topic; say who/how many people you interviewed; make sentences to illustrate the most interesting/relevant findings; conclude by saying if the data supports/disproves the ideas you had before you carried out the survey.

8. Share your texts with other groups. Ask if the categories are adequate and the sentences are clear. Make changes based on their feedback if necessary.

9. Print the final version of your work. Then tell your classmates what you have learned, using the charts and your paragraph.

10. With your classmates, group the charts and texts by topic and make a public exhibition.

11. Publish your work on the **Students for PEACE Social Media** <www.studentsforpeace.com.br>, using the tags **chart** and **paragraph** or others chosen by the students.

Peace talk

Chapters 1 and 2
Promoting gender equality

1 Look at this banner and talk to your classmates about the questions.

5 GENDER EQUALITY

a What do the three elements that make up the symbol on the right represent?

b Why do you think this is an often-discussed topic all over the world? In your opinion, how relevant is this topic?

c This banner is part of an important document. Do you know what document it is?

> **Going further**
>
> The **Sustainable Development Goals (SDGs)** are a set of universal goals that the United Nations adopted in September 2015. The objective is to end poverty, protect the planet and guarantee that all people, without discrimination, enjoy peace and prosperity. The SDGs include 17 goals that should be reached by 2030 all over the world.

2 Another document of worldwide importance is the Universal Declaration of Human Rights. Read an excerpt from one of its articles. Then relate it to the banner in activity 1 and answer the questions.

Article 13

"Everyone has the right to freedom of movement [...]."

ROOSEVELT, Eleanor et al. *Universal Declaration of Human Rights*. Bedford: Applewood Books, 2001. p. 4.

a What is the equivalent sentence in Portuguese?

b Why do you think this picture was chosen to illustrate the concept of this sentence?

3 In most societies, everyone has the right to freedom of movement, but it is known that women experience this freedom differently when they access public spaces. Read the text and understand why this happens. Do you agree with the author? Discuss.

> Street harassment has existed since the advent of streets, but for centuries it has been an overlooked problem. Today, men and women compete for equal access to public space – an area of our culture traditionally dominated by men. With the same tactics of intimidation and fear used when women demanded the right to own property, vote and enter every occupation, men have become more overt in oppressing women's right to access public spaces. Consequently, women have learned to fear the streets.

KEARL, Holly. **Stop Street Harassment:** Making Public Places Safe and Welcoming for Women. Santa Barbara: ABC-CLIO, 2010. p. XI.

> **Language clue**
> **Harassment** is a noun formed from the verb **to harass**, which means to bother or trouble someone, often in an aggressive act of intimidation.

4 This poster is an example of ways women around the world have found to combat street harassment. How important do you think initiatives like this are? Do you think you can also influence people to change their attitude in order to build a more respectful world for everyone?

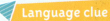

5 Although women harassment still is an under-reported practice, technology has been helping people around the world fight against it. Work in groups and do some research on this topic.

  a Find out how technology has been used around the world to combat harassment against women. Find out, for example, what apps have been developed, what they can do, how they are used etc. Check the quality and validity of the information you get.

  b Present your findings to your classmates, so that everyone gets to know more tools and starts using them to combat street harassment.

3 Citizenship

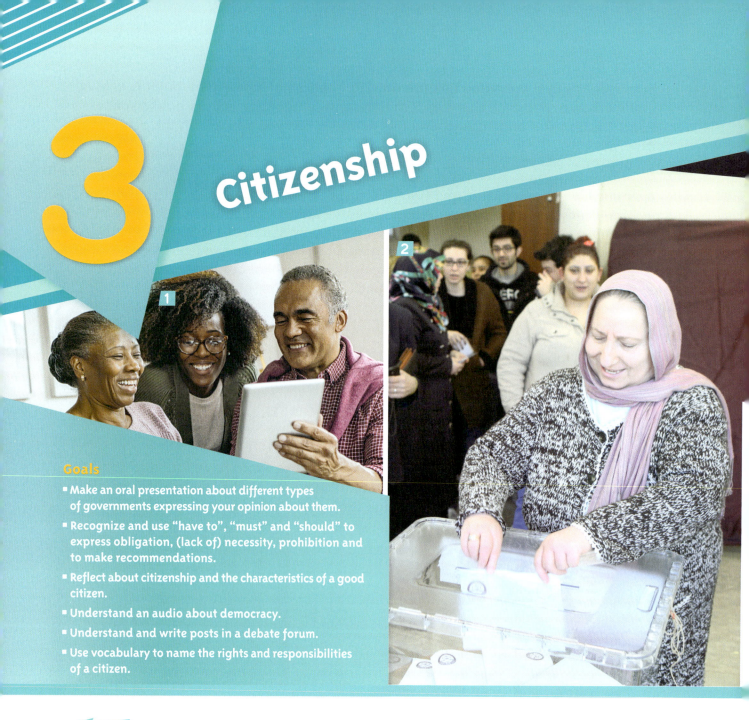

Goals
- Make an oral presentation about different types of governments expressing your opinion about them.
- Recognize and use "have to", "must" and "should" to express obligation, (lack of) necessity, prohibition and to make recommendations.
- Reflect about citizenship and the characteristics of a good citizen.
- Understand an audio about democracy.
- Understand and write posts in a debate forum.
- Use vocabulary to name the rights and responsibilities of a citizen.

Spark

1 What do you see in the pictures? Number these descriptions.

☐ Someone teaching other people to use a tablet.
☐ People doing volunteer work.
☐ A person holding his personal documents.
☐ A person voting in a political election.
☐ People protesting in the streets.

> **Language clue**
>
> **Citizenship:** the status of being a member of a particular country and having rights and responsibilities because of it.

2 Citizenship is about rights and responsibilities. Match the columns.

If you have a right to...   then you also have the responsibility...

a elect your leaders,

b a clean environment,

c be educated,

d a full life,

e freedom of thought, conscience and religion,

☐ to help so that the disadvantaged and the victims of discrimination have the chance to enjoy this right too.

☐ to choose your candidates carefully.

☐ to learn and share what you learn with others.

☐ to do what you can to look after your planet.

☐ to respect other's thoughts or religious principles.

Based on <https://en.wikisource.org/wiki/Universal_Declaration_of_Human_Responsibilities>. Accessed on May 10, 2019.

3 In your opinion, what rights and responsibilities in activity 2 are represented in the pictures? Do we have these rights and responsibilities in our society?

L1

Explore Forum post

Pre-reading

1 Answer these questions.

a Have you ever participated in an online discussion forum? What was it about?

_____

b Would you like to participate in a public discussion forum about…

☐ games?   ☐ music?   ☐ cinema?   ☐ fashion?   ☐ human interest topics?

2 Observe the forum post in activity 3. Then check the elements it contains.

☐ The page is divided into "Yes" and "No".   ☐ Thumbs up and thumbs down.
☐ The initial question that guides the discussion.   ☐ The name of the participants.

Reading

3 Read some comments on a forum post. Who do you agree with?

Do young people show enough respect to their elders?

👍 31% Say Yes   69% Say No 👎

1 **Age discrimination is wrong.** Age has absolutely nothing to do with how much respect you get. I am a middle school student and when a kid tries to defend themselves from a teacher's accusation, adults see it as back talk. To me, there's nothing wrong with back talk and we all have the right to stand up for ourselves.

2 **Yes, especially considering how the older generation treats us.** They blame us for LITERALLY EVERYTHING. It's not a matter of respecting your elders. You respect me, I'll respect you. It's as simple as that ;)

3 **They are revered.** Yes, young people show enough respect to their elders because they really appreciate what their ancestors have done.

4 **I was fired after 28 years because of disrespectful young people.** The young folks made fun of me; they would exaggerate mistakes I made. Why? Because young people don't want to listen to elders. They think they know it all.

5 **Children are spoiled.** I am a young adult and I think my people are very cruel to the elderly. I believe that a reform in the education system is necessary to instill respect for others, especially the elders.

6 **I do not think young people show enough respect to elders.** I think kids should start showing respect to their elders. Some kids are super rude these days. I do think that elders should show respect also. You're not going to get respect if you're an angry old person yelling at kids.

Adapted from <http://www.debate.org/opinions/do-young-people-show-enough-respect-to-their-elders>. Accessed on May 10, 2019.

4 Read the text again and check the appropriate options.

a The main objective of this forum is to discuss whether…
- [ ] elders have to be respected or not.
- [ ] young people respect the older generations or not.

b The participants who answered "Yes" seem to…
- [ ] totally agree with each other.
- [ ] have different points of view.

c By reading the comments under "No", it is possible to say that…
- [ ] some participants are young.
- [ ] all participants could be considered "elderly".

d According to the percentages, most participants think the young…
- [ ] do not respect their elders.
- [ ] show enough respect to their elders.

5 Read each comment again. Then write *T* (true) or *F* (false).

a [ ] In comment 1, the participant thinks that back talk is not disrespectful.

b [ ] In comment 2, the participant thinks that we should respect everybody, even if they do not respect us.

c [ ] In comment 3, the participant states that young people respect their elders.

d [ ] In comment 4, the participant says that young coworkers were nice to him/her.

e [ ] In comment 5, the participant mentions that he/she thinks it is necessary to change education to improve the way some young people treat their elders.

f [ ] In comment 6, the participant gives his/her opinion about how the elderly should behave.

6 Read the comments again and circle the appropriate options according to this forum's characteristics.

a Language: **formal**/**informal**
b Kind of post: **public**/**anonymous**
c Opinion poll: **present**/**not present**
d Information about the participants: **present**/**not present**
e Source of information: **reliable**/**unreliable**

> **Going further**
> In ancient Rome, the word *forum* described the public place where commercial, economic, political and social activities occurred. Research the similarities and the differences between a Roman forum and an online one. Then share your findings with your classmates.

7 Scan comments 1, 4, 5 and 6 in activity 3. Underline examples of what young people do/did that may disrespect the elderly.

Post-reading

8 Discuss this question with your classmates.

a Which behaviors that you have underlined in activity 7 have you already seen happen? How did the old person feel (sad, depressed, angry, didn't mind, normal, disappointed) in that situation? How did you feel about it?

L2

Expressing obligation and recommendation
Toolbox ("have to", "must", "should")

1 Read this post from a Q&A (question and answer) website and write *T* (true) or *F* (false).

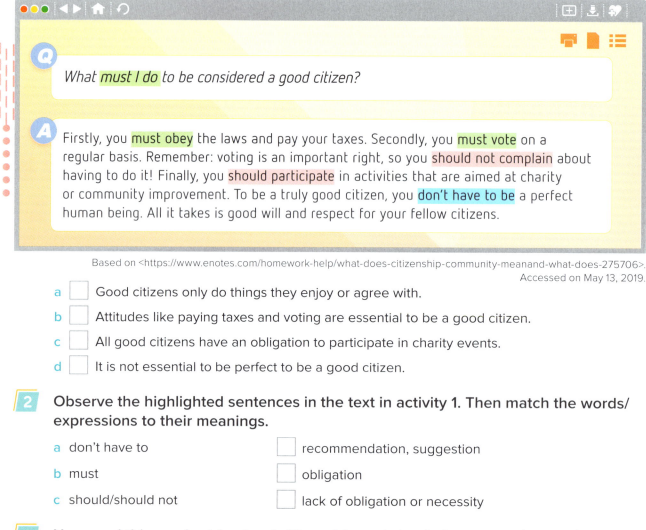

Based on <https://www.enotes.com/homework-help/what-does-citizenship-community-meanand-what-does-275706>.
Accessed on May 13, 2019.

a ☐ Good citizens only do things they enjoy or agree with.
b ☐ Attitudes like paying taxes and voting are essential to be a good citizen.
c ☐ All good citizens have an obligation to participate in charity events.
d ☐ It is not essential to be perfect to be a good citizen.

2 Observe the highlighted sentences in the text in activity 1. Then match the words/expressions to their meanings.

a don't have to   ☐ recommendation, suggestion
b must   ☐ obligation
c should/should not   ☐ lack of obligation or necessity

3 Now read this comic strip about citizenship and check the appropriate option.

Herb is doing community service because it is…

☐ an obligation.   ☐ a fun activity.

4 Read another comic strip related to obligations and complete the sentences.

a The elderly couple has _____ to help them clean the carpet.

☐ someone ☐ a robot

b When the lady says "[...] we didn't have to lift a finger.", she means _____ to help with the cleaning.

☐ it was necessary to do something ☐ it was not necessary to do anything

5 Read the texts in this section again and circle the appropriate options to complete the information in this box.

TALKING ABOUT OBLIGATIONS

- To talk about obligations, we can use "have to" or "**should**"/"**must**".
- To form questions and negatives with "have to", we **use/don't use** the auxiliary "do"/"does" (present) or "did" (past).
- To form questions with "must", we **use/don't use** the auxiliary "do"/"does" (present).
- **Must/Have to** cannot be used in the past.

ATTENTION! "MUST NOT" VS. "NOT HAVE TO"

You **must not swim** in the lake. = It is not permitted to swim in the lake.
You **don't have to swim** if you don't want to. = It's not necessary or obligatory that you swim if you don't want to.

6 Use the prompts to make sentences about what you see as obligatory, advisable or unnecessary.

a I/eat healthier. _____

b In my community, young people/respect the elderly. _____

c My neighbors/make less noise. _____

d My family/be eco-friendlier. _____

e Dog owners/clean up after their dogs. _____

L2

Building blocks Rights and responsibilities

1 Look at the pictures and match them to the attitudes described.

- [ ] Pay taxes.
- [ ] Buy and/or use pirated products.
- [ ] Litter the streets.
- [ ] Respect traffic laws.
- [ ] Cross the road while distracted.
- [ ] Respect priority seats.
- [ ] Help people in need.
- [ ] Know the law.

2 Use some of the phrases in activity 1 to complete these statements about citizenship.

a You shouldn't _____ because a car or a bike may hit you.

b You shouldn't _____ because paper may get into the drainage system and block it.

c All citizens must _____ so that the government can provide public services.

d All drivers, bikers and pedestrians must _____.

e We should always _____ when riding on public transportation.

f To demand respect for your own rights, you have to _____.

3 Complete this chart using the words in the box to list the rights and responsibilities of citizens. Then compare your ideas to your classmates'.

education   freedom of expression   freedom of thought, belief and religion
mobility   obeying the laws   paying taxes   respecting diversity
respecting the rights and beliefs of others   voting

RIGHTS

RESPONSIBILITIES

4 Discuss these questions with your classmates.

a Can you give more examples of a citizen's rights and responsibilities?

b Have you ever done anything that made your community, city or country a worse place? Why must these actions be avoided?

c What do you usually do to be a good citizen? What other things could you do to be a better citizen?

Watch:
Digital citizenship

L3

Sync Listening: Democracy

Pre-listening

1 How much do you know about politics? Do the following.

a Match each kind of government to who has the power in it.

I democracy
II monarchy
III oligarchy
IV tyranny

☐ a small group of people
☐ every citizen
☐ someone who takes control with power
☐ the king or the queen

b Check the appropriate option to complete this statement: About the concept of democracy, it is inaccurate to say that it...

☐ started in Greece.
☐ means the power of the people.
☐ has not changed throughout history.

Listening

2 🎧 7 Listen to the introduction of a class and write T (true) or F (false).

a ☐ The audio is going to talk about monarchy in the United States.
b ☐ Greece started as a democratic city-state.
c ☐ There were different types of government in Greece.
d ☐ Democracy in Greece influenced the United States.

3 🎧 7 Listen again. Take notes to complete this summary. Use the types of government in activity 1.

Athens started as a _____. Then the rich landowners took over and it became an _____. Eventually, some very powerful individuals overthrew that regime and established a _____. Then the people in Athens created a style of government called _____, in which people get to vote on the laws that govern them.

42

4 🎧 8 **Now listen to the second part of the class. Underline the option that states the main idea the teacher defends in the audio.**

> **There isn't much difference/There are many differences** between the democracy in the United States and the one originated in Athens.

5 🎧 8 **Listen again and take notes to complete this chart comparing democracy in Athens and in the United States.**

DEMOCRACY

	In Athens (Greece)	In the United States
Kind of democracy	_____ democracy.	_____ democracy.
People involved	Only male _____ got together to debate and vote laws.	Voters elect _____ to represent them.
Structure	_____ division of power.	Three branches: • _____ (to make the laws); • _____ (to enforce laws); • _____ (to interpret the laws and judge if people are innocent or guilty).
Electorate	Just free _____ (women, slaves and people who were not from Athens couldn't vote).	_____, _____ and immigrants who get _____.

Post-listening

6 **Discuss these questions with your classmates.**

a In your opinion, what are the advantages and disadvantages of each kind of democracy mentioned in the audio? Why?

b Do you think that one citizen has the power to change his/her society and government? Why?

c Why is it important to vote well in a representative democracy?

d Do you think people study the candidates before voting in an election? In your opinion, what should a citizen know about a politician before voting for him/her?

L3

Sync Speaking: Democracy and other types of governments around the world

Pre-speaking

1 Research the different types of governments and take notes.

2 Work in groups. Choose one type of government to present to the class. Find out which countries have adopted this system. Then collect information to answer these questions about two of the countries you have found out.

  a What are the main citizens' rights and duties? What are the good and the bad aspects of this type of government?

  b What are the similarities and differences between how the two countries handle this form of government?

3 Compare the information you have collected and what you know about the regime in your country. Find the answers to these questions.

  a What are the differences between the government in these countries and in your country?

  b What is your opinion about the situation in the countries you have studied?

4 Prepare a script for your presentation. Use data, pictures, maps and other resources to help you present your arguments. Remember to include your opinion about the type of government you chose.

Speaking

5 Make your presentation. Follow the instructions.

  a Introduce your presentation: mention the type of regime and the countries you will talk about.

  b Make your presentation.

  c Invite your classmates to give their opinion on the type of government you presented. Listen to their arguments and take notes in order to better explain your point of view in your turn.

  d Present your point of view in relation to your classmates' opinions in a respectful way.

  e Use the "Useful language" box to help you discuss the views and express your ideas.

> **Useful language**
>
> **Giving your opinion**
> In my opinion, …
> It seems to me that…
> I think that…
>
> **Clarifying**
> What I mean is…
> In other words, …
>
> **Agreeing**
> Exactly!
> That's true.
>
> **Interrupting**
> Excuse me, but…
> Sorry for interrupting, but…
> May I ask a question?
>
> **Disagreeing**
> I don't quite agree with you.
> I would disagree with that.
> I see your point, but…

Post-speaking

6 Which presentation did you like best? Why?

> **What:** a forum post
> **To whom:** other students; teachers; the community
> **Media:** paper; digital
> **Objective:** talk about an issue that is relevant for the community

1. In your opinion, what problems in your community need a solution? Make a list. Then share it with your classmates.

2. As a class, choose one problem to discuss in a public forum.

3. Review the characteristics of forum posts in the "Explore" section. Look for vocabulary and expressions you can use to discuss the problem. Take notes.

4. Decide if you are going to create a debate on an online forum or on a bulletin board. Write down a yes-no question to start the discussion in the forum.

5. Individually, write your answer to the question, explaining your opinion about the problem. Use examples and data to defend your point of view.

6. Exchange posts with a partner and ask him/her to check if the arguments are clear and if the post has a logical organization. Make comments on his/her post. Use the feedback to make any necessary changes in your text.

7. Post your comment on the forum.

8. Read the comments on the forum post. How many classmates agree with you? How many disagree? Write the percentage of opinions.

9. Publish your work on the **Students for PEACE Social Media** <www.studentsforpeace.com.br>, using the tag **forumpost** or others chosen by the students.

4 Sustainability

Goals

- Create an oral testimonial about initiatives related to sustainability.
- Learn some verbs used to describe environmental impact and how to reduce it.
- Reflect on which daily attitudes help protect the planet and which ones may harm it.
- Review the use of the modals "should", "have to" and "must" to express recommendation, necessity or obligation.
- Understand and create infographics about the environment and sustainability.
- Understand and use the modals "may", "might" and "will" to express probability.
- Understand oral testimonials.

Spark

1 What do the pictures show? Match them to the corresponding descriptions.

- [ ] A pile of trash in a landfill.
- [ ] Four color-coded recycling bins for different materials.
- [ ] A group of people/volunteers collecting trash.
- [ ] Plastic bottles floating in a river.
- [ ] Someone wasting food.

2 Which of the pictures represent "green attitudes", that is, actions that can affect the environment positively and contribute to sustainable global development? Support your answer.

L1

3. Which of the pictures show attitudes that can affect the environment negatively? Support your answer.

_____
_____
_____

4. Access to clean water is a topic that can be related to picture 4. Does everybody have access to clean water? Talk to your classmates.

47

L1

Explore Infographic

Pre-reading

 Look at the texts in activity 2 and check the appropriate options.

a Where do you usually find these infographics?

☐ On specific internet sites.   ☐ In biographies.
☐ In fiction books.   ☐ In magazines or newspapers.

b What is the possible reason why people read such infographics?

☐ Only to keep up to date with graphic design trends.
☐ To quickly understand key information about the matter.
☐ To get information for academic research.

Reading

2 Read texts 1 and 2. Then check the appropriate columns.

Text 1

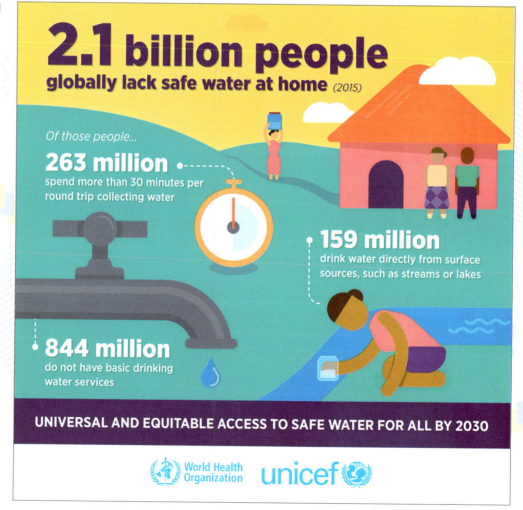

Available at <http://www.who.int/water_sanitation_health/monitoring/coverage/water2017-930px.jpg?ua=1>. Accessed on June 10, 2019.

48

Text 2

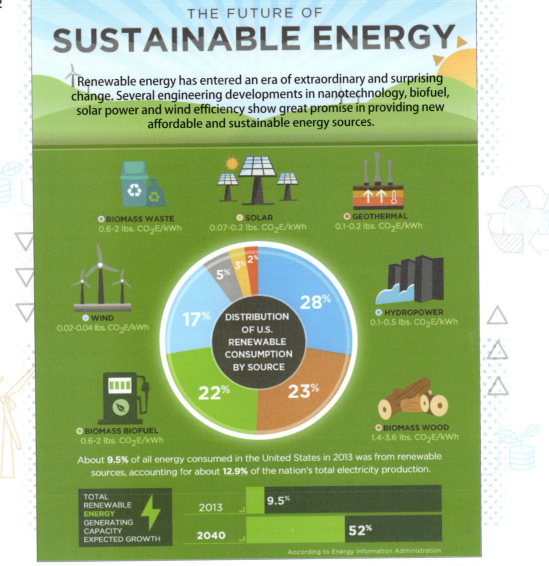

Available at <https://inhabitat.com/infographic-the-exciting-future-of-sustainability/>.
Accessed on June 10, 2019.

	Text 1	Text 2
a It depicts a universal problem without mentioning a specific country.		
b It is about a specific place in the world.		
c It was created by two entities with global authority to influence decision-makers.		
d It includes percentages.		

3 Complete the sentences according to text 1.

a The picture of a stopwatch helps us understand the fact that _____.

b The picture of a faucet helps us understand the fact that _____.

c The picture of a woman drinking water from a small narrow river helps us understand the fact that _____.

49

L1

4 Does the sum of the numbers related to three situations shown in text 1 equal the total number of people who lack safe water globally? Explain.

5 Now answer these questions according to text 2.

a What was the percentage of energy consumed from renewable sources in 2013 in the United States? What can you infer about the rest of the energy consumed?

b What kind of energy sources do the pictures represent? What are they?

c What was the most used source of renewable energy in the United States in 2013? And the least used one?

d What is expected to happen in the United States over the next two decades in terms of renewable sources?

6 Read the texts again and underline the appropriate options to complete the sentences.

a Both texts use a combination of **verbal language and pictures/verbal language and graphs** to present relatively complex information.

b Each text presents **a complete analysis with different points of view on the topic/information about a subject**.

c **There is some/There isn't any** statistical information in the texts.

d The use of colors in text 2 is **more/less** important for comprehension than in text 1.

e The main objective of both texts is to **inform and explain something/discuss an issue**.

Going further

When reading infographics, it is important to identify where the information comes from or who is responsible for its content in order to make sure of the credibility of the data.

Post-reading

7 Discuss these questions with your classmates.

a What pieces of information provided by texts 1 and 2 were new to you? Did any data surprise you? If so, which one and why?

b In your opinion, what is the importance of encouraging the use of renewable energy sources?

c What do you know about the use of renewable energy sources in your country?

Toolbox — Modals of probability ("may", "might", "will")

1 Read some excerpts about food loss and waste. Then answer the questions accordingly.

Excerpt I
"What is clear is that few countries have a positive waste management policy involving significant waste valorisation (although reliable data are not easily available from developing countries other than anecdotal evidence that in some countries such as India many people may make a basic living from collecting and selling waste)." (p. 3)

Excerpt II
"Recently, in France as well, supermarkets will be banned from throwing away or destroying unsold food and must instead donate it to charities or for animal feed [...]." (p. 231)

Excerpt III
"[...] waste management should occur according to the following hierarchy: reduce, reuse, recycle, recover energy and dispose." (p. 264)

Excerpt IV
"Considering that biomass is a renewable but limited resource whose production requires land and supplemental resources, it is important to analyse the demand for biomass in relation to the existing supply potential, land availability, expected technological trends, societal challenges and the fulfillment of the United Nations (UN) Sustainable Development Goals (SDGs). For achieving this, forward-looking policy decisions have to be made about the most appropriate use of available natural resources." (p. 182)

Excerpt V
"Foresight analysis represents an important tool for identifying and anticipating needs and challenges that might prevent an efficient and full deployment of a sustainable bioeconomy." (p. 169)

MORONE, Piergiuseppe; PAPENDIEK, Franka; TARTIU, Valentina Elena. **Food Waste Reduction and Valorisation: Sustainability Assessment and Policy Analysis.** Cham: Springer International Publishing, 2017.

a Where were the excerpts taken from?

b How do most countries deal with waste?

c What will supermarkets have to do with food that is not sold in France?

d What is the hierarchy of actions that have to be taken to avoid food waste?

e Why can we say that biomass as a renewable resource has its limitations?

L2

2 Complete the sentences according to the excerpts in activity 1.

a The modal that expresses the idea of recommendation is _____, as in excerpt _____.

b The modals that express the idea of probability (not so certain to happen) are _____, as in excerpts _____.

c The modals that express the idea of obligation are _____, as in excerpts _____.

d The modal that expresses the idea of probability (certain to happen) is _____, as in excerpt _____.

Going further

There is no significant difference between "may" and "might": both can express probability. In American English, "may" is more formal, so people who use this variant tend to say or write "might" (or "could") in everyday life. Some grammarians explain that "might" suggests a slightly lower degree of probability than "may", as the following examples illustrate:

Animals may have an intestinal blockage from eating marine plastic (= intestinal blockage is a possible consequence of eating marine plastic).

People might get sick by consuming seafood or fish that eat marine plastic (= it is slightly possible that people will get sick by consuming seafood or fish that eat marine plastic).

3 Think about your habits. Do you waste food in your house? If so, what could you do to avoid it? Write sentences using some of the given ideas.

- ✓ Shop smart and realistically.
- ✓ Don't over-serve food. Serve the right amount for yourself.
- ✓ Save uneaten food and actually eat it later.
- ✓ Store food in appropriate places.
- ✓ Keep food neat and visible in the refrigerator.
- ✓ Keep track of what you throw away to avoid doing it again.
- ✓ Donate food to food banks.
- ✓ Use helpful apps to learn new things about food waste.

Based on <https://mashable.com/2015/02/15/food-waste-tips/>. Accessed on May 12, 2019.

Building blocks — Verbs to describe environmental impact and how to reduce it

1 Look at some actions that can harm the planet. What are their consequences? Complete the sentences using the options from the box.

> cause land pollution   contribute to agricultural scarcity   destroy the forests
> kill water animals   pollute the air with the emission of CO_2 (carbon dioxide)
> produce greenhouse gas emissions

a Car engines _____ .

Specialists say this increases global warming.

b Food waste can _____ .

c Water waste limits water availability for other communities that depend on it for drinking, cleaning, cooking or growing food. This may also _____ .

d Deforestation may _____ .

e Excessive trash usually goes to landfills and may _____ .

f Plastic bags might end up in the oceans, rivers and lakes and _____ .

53

L2

2 Read this text about ways to help protect the planet. What should people do to preserve the environment? Check the options that reflect the ideas presented in the text.

Available at <https://oceanservice.noaa.gov/ocean/earthday.html>. Accessed on June 10, 2019.

☐ Reduce the amount of trash you produce.
☐ Turn off all daytime running lights.
☐ Use plastic bags only if they are made from recycled plastic bottles.
☐ Reduce car use, riding a bicycle instead whenever possible.
☐ Volunteer for cleanups in their communities.
☐ Avoid eating seafood as much as possible.

Watch: **Sustainability**

3 Read the text from activity 2 again and do the activities.

a Write the verbs (and their complements if necessary) that express actions people have to take to protect the planet.

b Which actions from item "a" should people take to solve the environmental problems caused by the actions presented in activity 1?

Sync Listening: Testimonials about helping the environment

Pre-listening

1 Look at the icons in activity 2. Cover their captions and guess what tip to help the environment each icon refers to.

Listening

2 🎧 9 Listen to the audio about a school in Australia. What are the kids' challenge in each excerpt? Write the numbers of the corresponding excerpts.

a
To plant veggies at school and feed their classmates.

b
To recycle old cell phones lying around their houses.

c
To exchange toys, games and books with classmates to reduce waste.

d
To save energy by turning off all the electrical stuff not in use.

3 🎧 9 Listen to the excerpts again and take notes in order to complete the texts.

1
In Australian houses, people have about _____ old mobiles lying around, and their parts could be recycled. The challenge of this group is to ask _____ in school to bring in their old mobiles and to pick them up in five minutes.
Mobiles have poisonous chemicals in them, and when they are chucked out with the garbage, these chemicals _____ water and soil and end up _____ .

2
The group has two challenges:
1. weed _____ and plant new veggies;
2. feed the _____ . On Tuesdays, local growers donate fruit and veggies for students, but, in this challenge, the students have to add food from their _____ .

3
This group's mission is based on the belief that _____ is one of the biggest planet warmers.

4
Most kids in Gabby's class want new toys, games and books, but they have things they _____ .
So, instead of throwing things away, the group has organized a 5-minute free _____ .

An Australian family of four generates seven tons of waste every year, which is a _____ more than what they did 10 years ago.

Post-listening

4 Which of the proposals to help change the world presented in the audio interested you the most? Why?

L3

Sync Speaking: Testimonial

Pre-speaking

1 Work in groups and follow the instructions.

a Think of an environmental problem that your school or community faces. Choose an action that can be taken in order to solve it and to contribute to world sustainability. Take notes.

b Discuss your ideas and decide on an action that can be taken to help the environment. This action needs to last five minutes and your group has to do it once a week at school.

c Every week, take notes about your activities. If possible, take pictures to keep track of what you are doing. If you get positive results, make sure to mention them in your notes.

d Prepare a written testimonial of your initiatives to help the environment at your school or in your community. Introduce yourselves and explain the problem you detected and the action taken to change it.

Speaking

2 Now present your experience orally to the other groups.

> **Useful language**
> In our group, we decided to…
> We noticed that in our community…
> In five minutes, we can…
> In ten weeks, it was possible to notice that…
> The results show…

Post-speaking

3 Discuss these questions with your classmates.

a How would you evaluate your experience in taking action to help the environment? What did you learn from it?

b How important were your classmates' actions to solve the problems they pointed out at school or in the community?

Studio Infographic

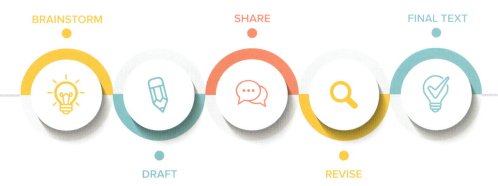

What: an infographic
To whom: other students; people in general
Media: paper; digital
Objective: explain an attitude that has to be avoided in your community in order to contribute to a sustainable environment

1. Review the infographics you have read in this chapter. What did you learn about this type of text? What pieces of information do you consider important to include?

2. In groups, think about an action that is harmful to the environment and should be avoided.

3. Research the reasons why this issue is relevant. For example, if you have thought of plastic bags, why should people stop using them?

4. Organize the information and plan how you are going to display it.

5. Create a draft of your infographic. Use the information collected and your ideas.

6. Share your draft with another group. Give some feedback on each other's drafts.

7. Make changes in your infographic based on the feedback you have received.

8. Share your infographic with your classmates.

9. Read the other groups' infographics. What did you learn about actions that are harmful to the environment? Do you think your five-minute action project from the previous section can help change this reality? If so, how?

10. Publish your work on the **Students for PEACE Social Media** <www.studentsforpeace.com.br>, using the tag **infographic** or others chosen by the students.

Peace talk

Chapters 3 and 4
We are born free and equal

1. Read Article 1 of the Universal Declaration of Human Rights. What are its main ideas? Discuss the questions with your classmates.

Article 1

"All human beings are born free and equal in dignity and rights."

ROOSEVELT, Eleanor et al. *Universal Declaration of Human Rights.* Bedford: Applewood Books, 2001. p. 2.

a What is the difference between this idea of equality and the idea of gender equality, studied in the previous "Peace talk"?

b What can be understood by the idea of being "free and equal"?

c How do you relate this article to the situation in your country? Are all people treated as free and equal in dignity and rights? Why?

2. Look at these pictures and answer the questions.

Some signs that dictated how people should live in South Africa under apartheid. This piece is part of the *Mandela: Struggle for Freedom* exhibit at the Canadian Museum for Human Rights, Winnipeg, Canada, on June 28, 2018

An apartheid sign on a beach near Hermanus, in the Cape Province, South Africa, December 1974

a What do these signs show? Where in the world were they displayed?

_____

b Would you believe that these signs existed if you didn't know about the problem they represent?

_____

c What do you know about the relation between Nelson Mandela and the apartheid?

d What do you know about the current situation in South Africa? If necessary, do some research into it.

3 What other segregation problems are still present in today's world? What do you think we could do in order to solve these problems?

4 Art is an important medium to raise awareness of human issues. Read this excerpt from a song by Bob Marley selected by Amnesty International to inspire social change. Then discuss the questions with your classmates.

> "Emancipate yourselves from mental slavery;
> None but ourselves can free our minds.
> Have no fear for atomic energy,
> 'Cause none of them can stop the time."
> "Redemption Song", by Bob Marley

a What is the message of this excerpt from the song?

b How can you relate this excerpt to Article 1 of the Universal Declaration of Human Rights?

c According to the song, to break free from mental slavery, we have to learn how to govern our own mind. Do you agree with this opinion? Explain.

Going further

In "Redemption Song", Jamaican artist Bob Marley (1945-1981) sums up what he always wanted to express in his lyrics: freedom. In this song, Marley refers to what Jamaican civil-rights activist Marcus Garvey (1887-1940) said in one of his speeches: "We are going to emancipate ourselves from mental slavery because whilst others might free the body, none but ourselves can free the mind."

5 Work in groups. Choose your own inspiring song to raise awareness of the importance of making a change in order to have a more equal and just society. Follow the steps.

a Search for songs related to social change, civil rights or citizenship.

b Choose one or more verses that show your concern. Write a short paragraph explaining the reasons for your choice.

c Present your inspiring song to your classmates. Explain why you have chosen it.

5 Global and local

Store decorated for Halloween in Tokyo, Japan

Restaurant offering food from different countries in Vashisht, India

Goals
- Identify the use of the present perfect to express actions that started in the past and extend into the present.
- Reflect on the interconnection between local and global situations, especially regarding languages, and on the positive and negative aspects of globalization, with a focus on cultural aspects.
- Understand a monologue defending an opinion.
- Understand and use expressions to present points of view, arguments and counterarguments.
- Understand and write an opinion article.

Spark

1 Answer these questions. Then discuss them with a partner.

a Which aspects of life does each picture represent: sports, celebrations, food or fashion?

b What connections can you make between the pictures, the content of the "Language clue" box and the title of this chapter?

Young women from different cultures together

Supporters from different countries together at a stadium

c What elements of other cultures are present in your lifestyle? Think about sports, food, entertainment, celebrations, technology, fashion etc.

_____

_____

Language clue

"In very broad terms, **globalization** is the worldwide integration of economic, technological, political, cultural and social aspects between countries."

HAMILTON, Sara M. ***Globalization.*** Edina: ABDO Publishing, 2009. p. 10.

L1

Explore Opinion article

Pre-reading

1 Test your knowledge about the African continent. Circle the appropriate options.

a In Africa there are **about 50/between 500 and 700/more than 2,000** languages.

b The main Portuguese-speaking African countries are **Angola and Mozambique/Nigeria and Liberia/Cameroon and Niger**.

c The African language that has the most learners as a second language (excluding French/English) is **Dinka/Berber/Swahili**.

Adapted from <https://www.freelang.net/mag/quiz04.php>. Accessed on April 25, 2019.

Reading

2 Read the title of the text. What do you think it is about? Discuss with a partner.

Global Agenda | Africa | Hyperconnectivity | Media, Entertainment and Information

IS LEARNING IN FORMER COLONIAL LANGUAGES A DISADVANTAGE FOR AFRICANS?

31 July 2015
Ernst Frederick Kotzé

In many African countries, French, English or Portuguese have been the languages of instruction in schools for decades. But there is evidence that this may not be the best for African societies.

In African schools, colonial languages are a medium of communication and a way to learn all school subjects. There are two reasons for that. Firstly, these languages are spoken worldwide, so they could be more useful in the long run. Secondly, a child will learn specific words like "decay" and "fault", which appear in science textbooks, but take on different meanings in common English. Therefore, children should be taught in a universal language to improve their understanding of content in other subjects.

However, research has proved that this has actually put generations of African children at a disadvantage. For example, in Burkina Faso, graduates from community schools who learned school subjects in the local language did better in a national exam than their peers from French language government schools. In Zambia, learners who studied in their home languages also outperformed their peers who learned all subjects in English. In both these cases, children learned French and English, respectively, only to communicate, not as a means to learn other school subjects. As a result, learners were more successful.

In conclusion, when deciding how to deal with language in education, it is important to keep our objectives clear and concentrate on what is possible to do. To restrict the objective of language learning to the access of knowledge in one field would be mixing up two separate objectives.

Author: Ernst Frederick Kotzé is Professor emeritus of Applied Language Studies at Nelson Mandela Metropolitan University.

Adapted from <https://www.weforum.org/agenda/2015/07/is-learning-in-former-colonial-languages-a-disadvantage-for-africans/>. Accessed on April 25, 2019.

3 Now read the text and check the best options.

a The text was written by a _____ .
☐ journalist   ☐ language specialist

b It is _____ publication.
☐ an online   ☐ a print

c It is _____ article.
☐ a news   ☐ an opinion

d Its purpose is to _____ about a subject.
☐ persuade the reader   ☐ be neutral

4 Read the text again. Use **[ ]** to indicate the parts of the text that present arguments for colonial languages at schools in Africa and **( )** to indicate the parts of the text that present arguments against it.

5 What type of argument does the author use to prove his point of view? Check the best option.

☐ He mentions facts from research on school exam results.
☐ He quotes students' opinions about this subject.

6 Circle the appropriate options to complete these inferences we can make based on the text.

a In Burkina Faso, **French/English** is the language of education in government schools.
b In Zambia, **French/English** is the language of education in government schools.
c In **community/government** schools, kids receive instruction in their local home language.
d The students who "outperformed" their peers did **better/worse** because they learned the subjects in their own language.

Post-reading

7 Discuss these questions with your classmates.

a In your opinion, why did those who studied in their home language do better in the research?
b How would you feel if the official language of education in Brazil was a global language, like English, Spanish or Mandarin?
c Do you think we will have only one global language in the future? Will local languages become extinct as the world becomes more interconnected?
d Is a language like English important for the advancement of sciences, trade and politics in a globalized world? Why?

Watch:
Hashtivism

L2

Building blocks Expressing points of view, arguments and counterarguments

1 Classify the highlighted words from the text on page 62 according to their function.

a Connectors used to express contrast: _____

b Connectors used to introduce and enumerate arguments: _____

c Connectors used to express consequence and result: _____

d Connectors used to give examples: _____

e Connectors used to express conclusion: _____

2 Read this extract from an online article and complete it with the appropriate connectors from activity 1.

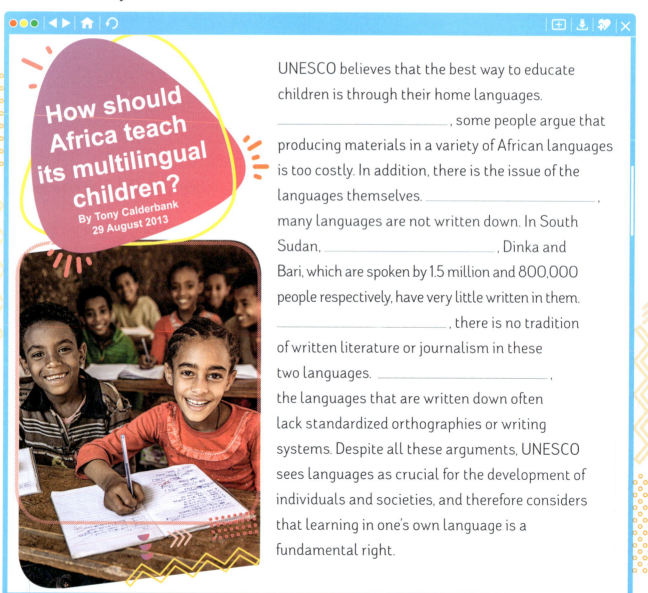

How should Africa teach its multilingual children?
By Tony Calderbank
29 August 2013

UNESCO believes that the best way to educate children is through their home languages. _____, some people argue that producing materials in a variety of African languages is too costly. In addition, there is the issue of the languages themselves. _____, many languages are not written down. In South Sudan, _____, Dinka and Bari, which are spoken by 1.5 million and 800,000 people respectively, have very little written in them. _____, there is no tradition of written literature or journalism in these two languages. _____, the languages that are written down often lack standardized orthographies or writing systems. Despite all these arguments, UNESCO sees languages as crucial for the development of individuals and societies, and therefore considers that learning in one's own language is a fundamental right.

Adapted from <https://www.britishcouncil.org/voices-magazine/how-should-africa-teach-multilingual-children>. Accessed on April 26, 2019.

3 Read the following extracts from a letter to the editor of *The New York Times*, which allows readers to follow a discussion on a specific subject. Which subject are people discussing: "globalization", "traditions" or "globalization and traditions"?

William V. Wishard's wrote

1 While we Americans believe that what works for America will work for all nations, we sometimes forget that cultural differences represent psychological differences. In my opinion, the critical question is: "How can we engage globalization without losing our traditions?"

Readers responded

2 Mr. Wishard poses an important question: "How can we engage globalization without losing our traditions?" To me, the answer is: we cannot. No one would deny that the process of globalization is significant. But we should not pretend that it can happen while preserving traditions.

David A. McM. Wilson

3 Mr. Wishard sees globalization as being about personal identity. I agree. However, while many people may relate to the idea of being global citizens, far too few are aware of what that implies.

Ron Israel
Adapted from *The New York Times*, New York, June 1, 2014.

4 Complete these sentences with *blue*, *green*, *pink* and *yellow* to explain how the writers present their points of view and the arguments/counterarguments to support them in the highlighted clauses in activity 3.

a The sentences in _____ introduce the writers' opinion.

b The sentences in _____ introduce the arguments (the reasons to support or oppose an idea) that the writer wants to contest.

c The sentences in _____ introduce the counterarguments (arguments that go against another argument) to defend the writer's points of view.

d The sentences in _____ refer to another participant's comment.

5 Write a short paragraph about one of the following topics, expressing your point of view and giving arguments for or against it. Use the language and the strategies you've seen in this section. Research the topic if necessary.

a We have become more open and tolerant towards each other.

b Globalization has led to the exploitation of labor.

c Globalization has caused environmental problems.

65

L2

Toolbox: Present perfect with "for" and "since"

1 Which aspect/s of globalization does each of these extracts focus on: cultural, economic or social? Read them and tell a partner.

a. Popular culture **has become** a part of everyday life for lots of people. For decades, western cultures **have influenced** other cultures. Their videos, music, jeans and shopping malls **have spread** in Asia, Africa and Latin America, but their influence, especially in the rural areas, is often limited. (p. 758)

b. Since colonial times, Africans **have exported** agricultural and mineral resources to the global economy, but this **hasn't been** a source of wealth for all the population in the continent. Sub-Saharan Africa **has had** the world's highest infant mortality rates, for example. (p. 890)

Adapted from LOCKARD, Craig A. *Societies, Networks, and Transitions:* A Global History. 2 ed. Stamford: Wadsworth Cengage Learning, 2011.

2 Analyze the highlighted clauses in activity 1 and check the appropriate options.

a. The highlighted clauses refer to actions that…
- [ ] started in the past and continue until the present.
- [ ] started and finished in the past.

b. All the clauses contain the auxiliary verb…
- [ ] do/does.
- [ ] have/has.

c. The main verbs are in the…
- [ ] present continuous (verb in the base form + -ing).
- [ ] past participle.

d. The negative is formed by adding "not" _____ the auxiliary verb.
- [ ] after
- [ ] before

3 Complete the chart with the verb forms in bold in activity 1.

Infinitive (base form)	Past simple	Past participle
export	exported	
influence	influenced	
have	had	
be	was/were	
become	became	
spread	spread	

4 Now complete the sentences with *yellow*, *pink*, *blue*, *green* or *gray* according to the chart in activity 3.

The verb/s in...

a _____ are regular verbs.

b _____ has the same form in the base form, in the past simple and in the past participle.

c _____ has different forms in the base form, in the past simple and in the past participle.

d _____ has the same form in the past simple and in the past participle, but it is different from the base form.

e _____ has the same form in the base form and in the past participle, but a different form in the past simple.

5 Complete these extracts with the appropriate form of the verbs in parentheses.

a Pop culture _____ a part of everyday life for billions of people for some time now, but no common world culture _____ so far. (be; emerge)

b Globalization _____ the lives of poor people in many countries. Besides, it _____ to continued foreign domination of some groups and nations by others. (not improve; lead)

c Industrialization _____ throughout Asia and Latin America. With that, the service and information industries _____ rapidly. (spread; grow)

Adapted from LOCKARD, Craig A. **Societies, Networks, and Transitions: A Global History.** 2. ed. Stamford: Wadsworth Cengage Learning, 2011.

6 Read this sentence and circle the appropriate options to complete the explanation.

> **Has** pop culture **been** a part of everyday life for billions of people for some time now?

To form the interrogative form, we place the auxiliary verb **after/before** the subject + the main verb in the **past participle/past simple**.

7 Read the excerpts in activity 1 again and circle the appropriate options.

a In the excerpts, "for decades" and "since colonial times" are expressions that indicate **time/place**.

b "Since" **comes before a point in time/indicates a period of time**.

c "For" **comes before a point in time/indicates a period of time**.

8 Answer these questions about yourself using *since* or *for*. Then talk to a partner.

a How long have you lived in your current neighborhood? _____

b How long have you studied English? _____

c How long have you known your best friend? _____

L3

Sync Listening: Global challenges

Pre-listening

1 Name the challenges represented in the pictures using the vocabulary from the box.

climate change   deforestation   nuclear weapons
poverty and starvation   terrorism

Listening

2 **10** Listen to Arthur Mutambara, a politician from Zimbabwe, answering this question: what are the world's greatest challenges? Then circle the best options.

a The politician is expressing his point of view on **climate change/terrorism**.
b He sees it as a **local/global** challenge.
c According to him, it is **an isolated problem/a challenge connected to other challenges**.
d His friends in other countries **share/don't share** his opinion.

68

3 🎧 **11** Listen to part 1 of the audio again. Then complete this mind map that shows how the challenges are interconnected, as mentioned in the audio.

4 🎧 **12** Listen to part 2 of the audio again and complete its transcript with the names of the countries.

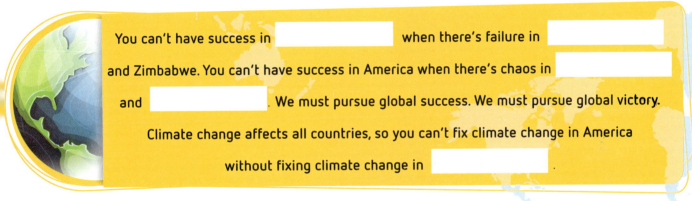

You can't have success in _____ when there's failure in _____ and Zimbabwe. You can't have success in America when there's chaos in _____ and _____. We must pursue global success. We must pursue global victory. Climate change affects all countries, so you can't fix climate change in America without fixing climate change in _____.

Post-listening

5 Answer these questions and discuss with a partner.

a Do you agree or disagree with Arthur Mutambara's opinion that global challenges are interconnected?

☐ I agree. We can't have progress in one country while there are other countries left behind.

☐ I disagree. Fighting terrorism, for example, is not a challenge in Brazil. So it isn't interconnected to our problems.

b In your opinion, is it possible for the world to come together as one, working for a "global victory", as Mutambara argues? Why?

☐ Yes. Globalization makes people more aware of the importance of working together for a better future.

☐ No. Some nations will always want to dominate and exploit others.

L3

Sync Speaking: A debate

Pre-speaking

1 Have you ever been in a debate? What are the roles people play in it? Read and match.

a affirmative team
b opposition team
c moderator
d audience

☐ Defends the subject/issue.
☐ Watches the debate.
☐ Opposes to the subject/issue.
☐ Conducts the debate, explains the rules, keeps track of who speaks, when and for how long, assesses the debate.

2 Let's prepare a debate.

a Decide who is going to be the moderator. Determine the debate rules with him/her.
b Get into groups. Choose one topic related to the theme "global and local".
c Choose sides: the affirmative team or the opposition team.
d Do some research on the topic and prepare your arguments according to your team.
e Review the "Building blocks" section for expressions to use in the debate.
f Prepare the script.
g Decide who is going to present each part of the argumentation.
h Practice with the members of your team. Make sure you follow the set speaker times.
i Make comments about your classmates' arguments and listen to their feedback about your speech. Make changes if necessary.

Speaking

3 Now you are going to conduct a debate.

Moderator
Greet the audience, introduce yourself and the issue under debate. Read the debate rules. Take turns introducing the speakers on the affirmative and on the opposition team until they all have had the opportunity to join the debate. At the end, thank the participants and highlight the best arguments.

Affirmative team
Introduce the topic and deliver your argument/s. Thank the audience at the end.

Opposition team
Choose one of the affirmative team's arguments to refute. Build your counterargument. Thank the audience at the end.

Post-speaking

4 Can this type of activity teach us about defending our positions while respecting those who think differently from us? Explain.

Studio Opinion article

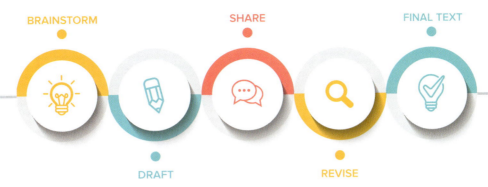

> **What:** an opinion article
> **To whom:** other students; people in general
> **Media:** paper; digital
> **Objective:** express your opinion about a global challenge

1. List some global challenges that are relevant to your community.
2. Choose one challenge to investigate. Find out what different groups of people think about it.
3. List the main arguments in each group. Decide on your position.
4. Organize the data according to points of view. Choose arguments to represent each side and give your opinion. Support them with quotes, data, examples etc.
5. Review the opinion article in the "Explore" section and the expressions in the "Building blocks" section.
6. Write the first draft. Make a general statement about the challenge. Then present the first argument, showing what each side thinks and your personal opinion. Support the ideas with facts and quotations. Repeat this step for the second argument. Finally, write a conclusion supporting your point of view.
7. Ask a classmate to read your article and say if the arguments and counterarguments sound logical and if your opinion is clear. Make changes if necessary.
8. Pin the final version of your article up on the classroom board for your classmates to read.
9. Group the articles under similar topics. Discuss the content and compare points of view. How have the texts enriched your views about the topics?
10. Publish your work on the **Students for PEACE Social Media** <www.studentsforpeace.com.br>, using the tag **opinionarticle** or others chosen by the students.

6 Consumer society

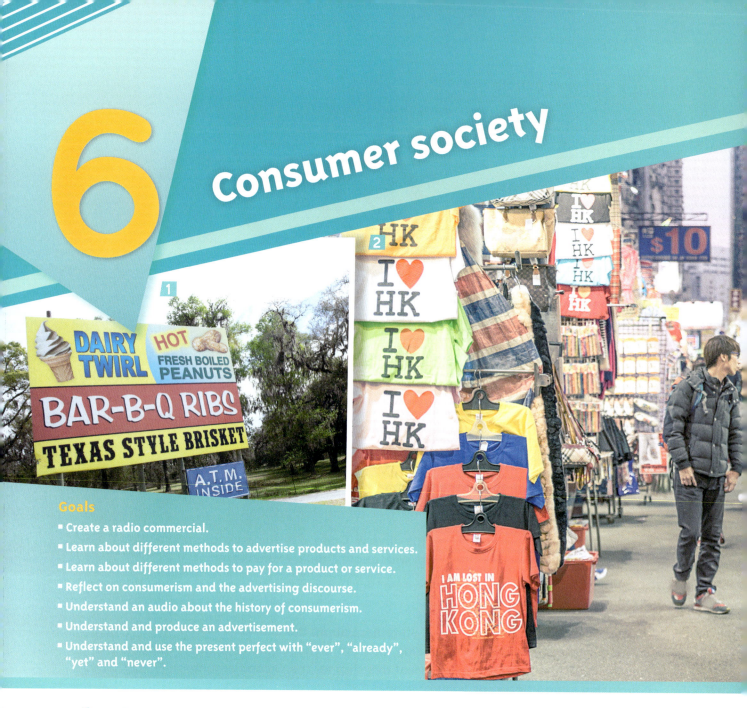

Goals
- Create a radio commercial.
- Learn about different methods to advertise products and services.
- Learn about different methods to pay for a product or service.
- Reflect on consumerism and the advertising discourse.
- Understand an audio about the history of consumerism.
- Understand and produce an advertisement.
- Understand and use the present perfect with "ever", "already", "yet" and "never".

Spark

1 Match the pictures to their descriptions.

- [ ] A shopping cart full of merchandise in a supermarket.
- [ ] A man looking at the products displayed at a street market.
- [ ] A "skip ad" button on a website.
- [ ] A work of art about consumerism.
- [ ] A billboard announcing different kinds of food.

2 Discuss the questions with your classmates.

a Which of the pictures best represents the sensation of being lost while facing too many options to buy? Explain.

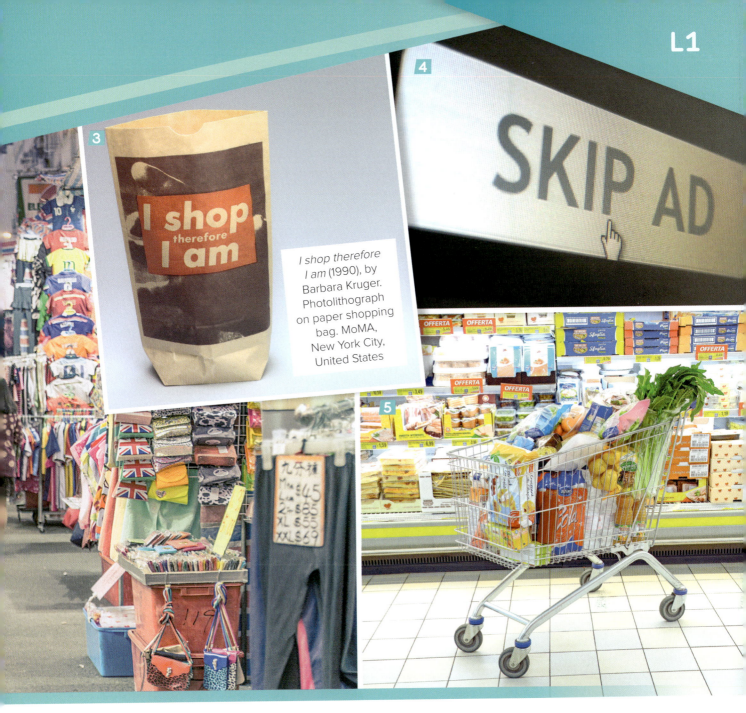

I shop therefore I am (1990), by Barbara Kruger. Photolithograph on paper shopping bag. MoMA, New York City, United States

b When you watch videos online, do you always skip the ads or do you sometimes watch them? Support your answer.

c Do you usually pay attention to ads on websites, magazines, TV, newspapers etc.? If so, do ads have the power to convince you to consume?

3 Look at picture 3, which was based on Descartes' proposition "I think, therefore I am". What was probably Barbara Kruger's intention in doing so? Why do you think the artist chose this object and this phrase? Check.

☐ She wanted to show that shopping is an essential activity for people. In order to be ecologically correct, she used a shopping bag made of recycled paper.

☐ She wanted to criticize people who buy too many things. She used a paper bag to show that what you put inside it is often as insubstantial as the bag.

☐ Other: _____

L1

Explore Advertisement

Pre-reading

1 Look at texts 1 and 2 and check the best option in each question.

a What type of text are they?
- [ ] advertisements
- [ ] editorials
- [ ] opinion articles
- [ ] photojournalism articles

b Who usually creates this type of text?
- [ ] advertising agencies
- [ ] editors
- [ ] journalists
- [ ] photographers

c Where did these texts probably circulate?
- [ ] In digital newspapers and magazines.
- [ ] In print newspapers and magazines.
- [ ] In both digital and print newspapers.
- [ ] Exclusively in magazines.

Text 1

Available at <http://www.aviationexplorer.com/airline_aviation_ads/pan-american-ad.htm>.
Accessed on June 10, 2019.

Text 2

Available at <https://witness2fashion.wordpress.com/tag/singer-sewing-machine-ads-1917-1937-1938-1939/>. Accessed on June 10, 2019.

> **Language clue**
>
> **Advertisement** (or **ad**) is a type of communication, often written, that someone pays to help promote and sell a product, a service, an idea etc. Advertisements aired on television or radio are called "commercials".
>
> **Advertising** is the business of creating advertisements, for example: advertising agency, advertising photographer, advertising industry etc.

Reading

2 Read texts 1 and 2. Who is the target audience of each ad? Check the most appropriate option in each column.

Text 1
- [ ] flight attendants
- [ ] travel agents
- [ ] aircraft mechanics
- [ ] pilots
- [ ] businesspeople and tourists

Text 2
- [ ] manufacturers of sewing machinery
- [ ] sewing machine technicians
- [ ] fashion models
- [ ] people who make or mend clothes
- [ ] typists

L1

3 Now write *T1* for text 1, *T2* for text 2 or *BT* for both texts.

a The objective is to encourage the target audience to buy...
  I   a service: _____
  II a machine: _____

b The information about the service/product includes...
  I   its price: _____
  II   a reference to guarantee: _____
  III its physical characteristics: _____
  IV   the name of the company that offers the service or makes the product: _____
  V   a place where one can buy the service or product: _____

c Verbal and non-verbal elements consist of...
  I   an adjective to say the product or service is modern or different: _____
  II   different shades of black, font sizes and types: _____
  III a picture as the biggest visual element in the ad: _____
  IV   a phrase expressing the idea that the company is there for the consumer: _____
  V   short sentences with the omission of the subjects: _____

4 Below are some characteristics of an effective ad. Read them and discuss: do the ads in texts 1 and 2 contain any of these characteristics? Check all possible options.

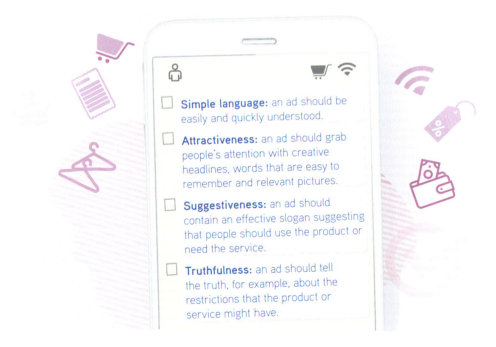

☐ **Simple language:** an ad should be easily and quickly understood.

☐ **Attractiveness:** an ad should grab people's attention with creative headlines, words that are easy to remember and relevant pictures.

☐ **Suggestiveness:** an ad should contain an effective slogan suggesting that people should use the product or need the service.

☐ **Truthfulness:** an ad should tell the truth, for example, about the restrictions that the product or service might have.

Post-reading

5 Discuss these questions with your classmates.

a If you needed to buy a service or a product, would an ad with the characteristics of texts 1 and 2 grab your attention? Why?

b Do you think an ad like the one in text 2 would be created nowadays? Why?

L2

Toolbox Present perfect with "ever", "already", "yet" and "never"

1 Look at the picture in activity 3. Does it represent an internet ad or a traditional TV commercial? Explain.

2 Do you watch TV very often? If so, are the ads shown on TV the same as those you see online?

3 Read this text and check if the statements are *T* (true) or *F* (false).

"[...] Advertising has become such an inextricable part of our lives — thanks to television — that we can't really imagine life without it. Is there a way to determine how much advertising affects our lives and influences our purchase decisions [...]? Besides, who monitors the subliminal and surrogate advertising that we hardly ever notice [...]? Are advertisers free to use any form of advertising and promotion to push their sales? Have you **ever** thought if there should be a line drawn between make-believe advertising and reality? [...]"

CHAUDHARY, Anjali Y. *The Impact of Television Advertising on Children.*
Solapur: Laxmi Book Publication, 2016.

a ☐ The text is about how advertising manipulates our choices and spending habits.
b ☐ The author presents some solutions for the problem she mentions.
c ☐ The author proposes some questions for the reader to consider.
d ☐ The book focuses on the problems faced by a target audience of a specific age group.
e ☐ The author compares television advertising to online advertising.

4 Read the text in activity 3 again, focusing on the highlighted verb forms. Then complete the sentences by checking the appropriate options.

a The verb form highlighted in yellow expresses...
   ☐ something that happened in a specific time in the past.
   ☐ something that was true in the past and that is still true in the present.

b The purpose of the verb form highlighted in blue and of the word in bold is to ask if something...
   ☐ usually happens in someone's life.
   ☐ has happened at any time in someone's life.

L2

5 Now read the following texts. Then complete the sentences with *already*, *ever* or *yet*.

Text 1

"**Have** you **ever noticed** that if you see an ad for a product in one place, you'll probably see ads for that same product in other places too?"

BODDEN, Valerie. *Identify and Evaluate Advertising.* Minneapolis: Lerner Publications, 2015. p. 12.

Text 2

"Look-alike modeling [...] finds consumers who exhibit similar online patterns to those consumers who **have** *already* **demonstrated** a desired behavior, or who **have** *already* **generated** a conversion on their site."

GOLD, Harry J. *The Digital Advertising Guide.* Allston: Overdrive Marketing Communications, 2015. p. 31.

Text 3

"Online advertising **has not** *yet* **come** to the point of perfection, and perhaps it never will."

TAYLOR, Gabriela. *Advertising in a Digital Age: Best Practices & Tips for Paid Search and Social Media Advertising.* Bexhill-on-Sea: Global & Digital, 2013. p. 15.

a _____ is used in **interrogative** sentences.

b _____ is used in **affirmative** sentences and it may suggest that something has happened sooner than expected.

c _____ is used in **negative** sentences and it suggests that something hasn't happened but may still happen.

6 Write questions following the example. Then, in pairs, answer the questions orally using *already*, *yet* or *never*.

a buy something because of an ad or a commercial

A: Have you ever bought something because of an ad or a commercial?

B: Yes, I have (already bought something because of an ad or a commercial).
No, I haven't (bought something because of an ad or a commercial yet).
No, I have never bought something because of an ad or a commercial.

b catch yourself humming or singing a commercial jingle

_____

c stop to have a better look at a creative billboard

_____

d cry because of an ad

_____

L2

Building blocks — Types of advertising and money vocabulary

1 What types of advertising do the pictures represent? Match them to the corresponding labels.

- a billboard
- b bus stop shelter advertising
- c celebrity branding
- d direct mail
- e newspaper
- f online/print magazine
- g sandwich board sign

Portuguese soccer player Cristiano Ronaldo endorsing an advertising campaign in Sydney, Australia

2 What other types of advertising can you think of?

79

L2

3 In your opinion, what is the most effective type of advertising to sell/promote the following items? Talk to a partner.

- houses/apartments
- medical insurance
- new cars
- pets
- rock concerts
- smartphones
- supermarket groceries
- toys
- travel programs

4 Look at the pictures that show different modes of payment and match them to their descriptions.

☐ Pay **cash** (using paper currency or coins).

☐ Pay by **check**.

☐ Pay with a **gift card**.

☐ Pay using an **automated teller machine (ATM)**.

☐ Pay by **credit card** or **debit card**.

5 Circle the appropriate options to complete the definitions.

a to pay out or use up money to buy things: **to save/to spend**

b to put some money aside as a reserve: **to withdraw/to save**

c to receive money from someone or from an institution with the purpose of returning it later: **to spend/to borrow**

d a charge for money we borrow, often a percentage of the amount borrowed per a certain period of time: **interest (rate)/installment**

e to take money from the bank where it was deposited: **to lend/to withdraw**

f one of the parts into which the value is split when we pay something at intervals: **installment/interest (rate)**

g to give money for short-term or long-term use on the condition that the same amount, or an equivalent, is given back after a certain period of time: **to lend/to borrow**

Sync Listening: The history of consumerism

Pre-listening

1 In your opinion, what is the difference between essential objects and luxury ones?

2 Imagine life in the beginning of the 18th century. In your opinion, which of these objects would people consider essential and which ones would they consider luxury?

a bowl · a broom · a comb · a mirror · a pan
a pillow · pots · a towel · boots · farming implements

Listening

3 🎧 13 Listen to the beginning of the audio that accompanies a video on the history of consumerism. How does the narrator describe what the majority of the Earth's inhabitants owned? Check.

☐ They had enough to live comfortably, although they were poor.
☐ They had more or less nothing.
☐ They had nothing, as everything belonged to the government.

4 🎧 13 Listen to the audio again and take notes to complete these statements.

a Clothes, bowls, pots, pans, brooms and farming implements were considered _____ items.

b The remarkable phenomenon of the economy expanding and wages rising occurred in Northwestern _____.

c Historians describe the period of epochal change as the world's first _____ revolution.

Post-listening

5 Electricity was once considered a luxury. Can you think of other things that were once luxury items and that are now considered essential?

L3

Sync Speaking: **Radio commercial**

Pre-speaking

1 Look at the picture of someone presenting a radio commercial. Which item from the ads in the "Explore" section is she promoting, based on the text?

Have you always wanted to travel around the world? Asia? South America? Or maybe you've always dreamed of visiting Africa? We can make your dream come true! We fly to 121 cities on 6 continents! Visit our website or call us now!

2 You are going to create a radio commercial. Follow the instructions.

a In groups, choose one of the ads from the "Explore" section to promote.

b List the features of your product/service. Choose the most relevant ones for the commercial.

c Review the characteristics of ads in the "Explore" section. Then read these six tips to create good radio ad campaigns.

→ Use captivating words and phrases with simple language.
→ Use the right words to grab your target audience's attention.
→ Use a jingle to quickly make people remember your product/service.
→ Speak with emotion and enthusiasm to be more convincing.
→ Be creative, even if you have to use the traditional format of radio ads.
→ Be short, but emphasize the qualities of your product/service.

d Write a script for your commercial. Make it last about 30-60 seconds.

e Share your script with other groups to get their feedback. Make the necessary adjustments.

f Rehearse. Decide if you will add special effects, music or any other element to make your commercial more interesting.

Speaking

3 Present your radio commercial to your classmates.

Post-speaking

4 Did you like your commercial? Would you do anything differently next time? Why?

Studio Advertisement

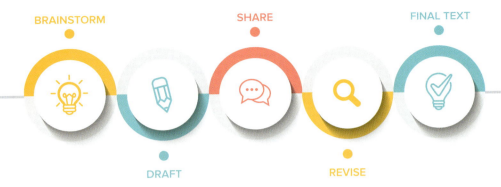

> **What:** an advertisement
> **To whom:** other students; people in general
> **Media:** paper; digital
> **Objective:** create an ad to promote/sell a product, service or idea

1. Work in groups. Brainstorm some possible products, services or ideas. Choose one to promote in your advertisement.
2. Review the characteristics of ads in the "Explore" section. Take notes. Decide if the ad is for a newspaper, a magazine or other types of print/digital media.
3. Write the text for the ad and decide if you are also going to use pictures.
4. Show your ad to other groups. Ask them for feedback. Make comments on their work as well.
5. Make the necessary adjustments.
6. Write the final version of your ad, adding the picture/s if you chose to use them. Remember to write the text in a variety of font types, colors and sizes to make the ad attractive.
7. Pin it up on the classroom board for your classmates to read.
8. Vote for the ad you like best, explaining why you prefer it.
9. Talk to your classmates about the advertising world. Would any of you like to pursue this career? Why?
10. Publish your work on the **Students for PEACE Social Media** <www.studentsforpeace.com.br>, using the tag **advertisement** or others chosen by the students.

Peace talk

Chapters 5 and 6
Happiness comes from within

1. Look at the pictures. What do you think they are calling our attention to? What is your attitude toward this situation? Discuss your ideas with your classmates.

2. Read the text. Then check the option that best summarizes this excerpt.

> During the course of this book, I share a number of inspiring lessons I've learned along the way. Those lessons include:
> - Happiness comes from connecting to your community and building strong relationships.

84

- Money can buy happiness, but it depends on how you spend it.
- The excessive consumption of material goods won't make you happy over the long run.
- Learning to get more from less is one way to find happiness, reclaim your time and live on your own terms.
- Any kind of life change requires hard work, patience and the willingness to be open to new perspectives.

Adapted from STROBEL, Tammy. **You Can Buy Happiness (and It's Cheap):** How One Woman Radically Simplified Her Life and How You Can Too. Novato: New World Library, 2012. p. 3-4.

a ☐ The text covers five useful tips for people who are trying to deal with the symptoms of compulsive shopping.

b ☐ The text covers some explanations about why some people think that happiness depends on external conditions.

c ☐ The text covers some lessons that the author has learned about happiness from things that she experienced in her own life.

3 By considering the text in activity 2, we can conclude that happiness does not depend on buying things and that it comes from connecting to the people around you. Do you agree? Explain.

4 What about happiness in your community? In groups, create a project related to the first lesson presented in the text in activity 2. Follow the instructions.

a Think about the problems your community is facing at the moment — for example, problems related to sustainability.

b Make a list of actions that should be taken by you, your community and your country as a whole to solve the problem. Use this chart as an example.

Me	My community	My country
Not to litter public spaces.	To create a campaign to make public spaces cleaner.	To promote recycling research.

c Discuss which actions should/must be implemented immediately and how they could be done. Start with small gestures that may bring greater consequences if followed by everyone.

d Present your ideas to your teacher and classmates. Then put your project into practice.

7 Fighting for our rights

Ditch full of sewage and garbage in a street in South Sudan

People standing in a crowded subway in Bangkok, Thailand

Goals

- Create an awareness campaign about people's rights.
- Discuss an issue related to human rights, presenting arguments and considering different points of view.
- Review and use the present simple, past simple and present perfect.
- Understand an interview about racism.
- Understand and use connectors (linking words).
- Understand the characteristics of a photojournalism article.
- Understand the characteristics of an awareness campaign.

Spark

1 Look at the pictures and number the social problems each of them illustrates.

☐ Violence in the community.
☐ Poor living conditions in the community.
☐ Insufficient public transportation for the population.
☐ Unemployment and homelessness.
☐ Lack of investments in health care.

2 Answer these questions. Then discuss with your classmates.

a Which of the problems represented in the pictures occur in your city?

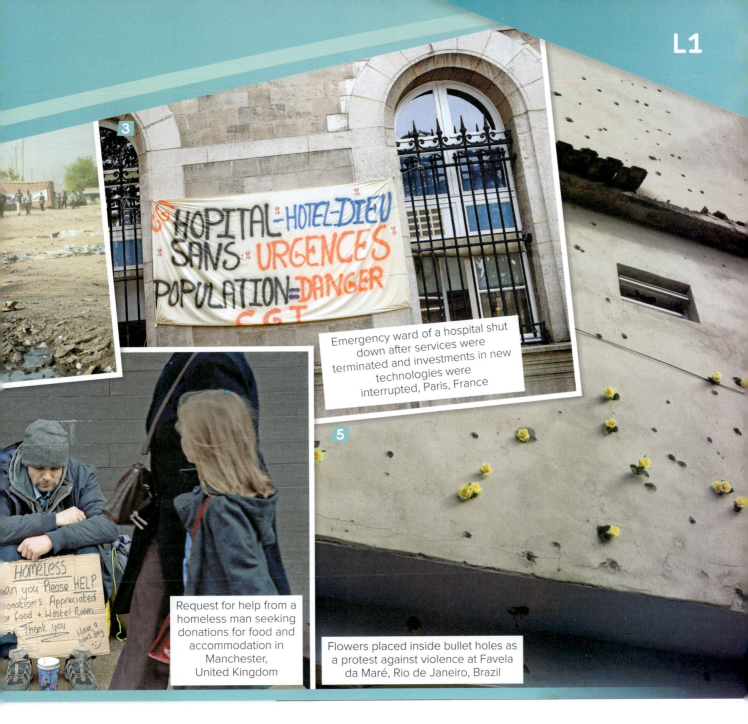

Emergency ward of a hospital shut down after services were terminated and investments in new technologies were interrupted, Paris, France

Request for help from a homeless man seeking donations for food and accommodation in Manchester, United Kingdom

Flowers placed inside bullet holes as a protest against violence at Favela da Maré, Rio de Janeiro, Brazil

b In your opinion, what are the risks and harms of living in such conditions?

3 Read this definition of "human rights". Then discuss with your classmates how knowing them can help us fight for our rights.

"Every person has certain fundamental rights guaranteed by law. These are called 'human rights'. For example, we all have the right to housing, medical care and education. We have the right to live in freedom and safety. We also have the right to do a job and get paid for it. Human rights are important to stop abuses such as discrimination, intolerance, injustice, oppression and slavery."

Adapted from <https://www.youthforhumanrights.org/what-are-human-rights/>. Accessed on May 16, 2019.

L1

 **Explore** Photojournalism article

Pre-reading

Watch:
Education in South Africa

 Look at the pictures in activity 2 and discuss the questions.

    a What is happening in the two pictures?

    b Do the man in a suit in picture 1 and the lady in a dress in picture 2 look aggressive?

    c Think about the title of this chapter. Why do you think these people are being arrested?

Reading

 Read this photojournalism article and the "Going further" box. Then write *T* (true) or *F* (false).

How Photographs Define the Civil Rights and Black Lives Matter Movements

Mark Speltz Sep. 22, 2016

Most Americans today learn about the Civil Rights Movement through images documenting speeches by charismatic leaders such as Martin Luther King, Jr., dramatic clashes between nonviolent marchers and the police and massive demonstrations. These incredibly powerful pictures, which once appeared in newspapers and magazines, now repeatedly appear in modern history textbooks and are critical touchstones in the visual narrative of our nation's past.

Civil Rights organizers knew that pictures could build sympathy for the cause, attract financial support and prod politicians to offer protection and, eventually, enact landmark legislation. Because of this, activists looked for the type of photographic coverage that not only showed the intensity of the struggle, but also made the massive resistance to change visible.

Pictures from Black Lives Matter protests resemble Civil Rights era photography and serve many of the same crucial roles: they document, preserve, provide evidence and inspire activism. Take for example the viral arrest photo of Ieshia Evans, the lone woman in a dress in Baton Rouge. These pictures represent only a millisecond of a long, contested struggle. Yet, as they are shared and broadcast online, they shape how we see and remember these events for years to come.

The gripping pictures documenting the Black Lives Matter movement have undoubtedly changed the course of our recent history, just as stirring Civil Rights era photographs did more than five decades earlier.

Adapted from <http://time.com/4429096/black-lives-matter-civil-rights-photography/>. Accessed on May 16, 2019.

L1

> **Going further**
>
> The **Civil Rights** movement (1954-1968) fought racial discrimination against African Americans. Martin Luther King, Jr. was an icon of this movement. The **Black Lives Matter** (2013-), in turn, is a movement that campaigns against violence and racism towards black people.

a ☐ The photojournalism article is about the importance of photography for both the Civil Rights and the Black Lives Matter movements.

b ☐ Photography does not have the power to influence public opinion.

c ☐ Photography proves that there are similarities between the Civil Rights and the Black Lives Matter movements.

3 Read the underlined sentences in the article. Do they present the main arguments in the text? Or evidence and examples that support the arguments in the text?

___

4 Match the pictures from the photojournalism article in activity 2 to their captions.

☐ A demonstrator protesting against the death of Alton Sterling, a 37-year-old black man killed by two police officers, is detained by law enforcement near the headquarters of the Baton Rouge Police Department in Baton Rouge, Louisiana, U.S., on July 9, 2016

☐ Police officers O. M. Strickland and J. V. Johnson apply force in arresting Reverend Martin Luther King, Jr. for loitering near a courtroom where one of his assistants was on the stand. King charged he was beaten and choked by the arresting officers. Police denied the charges. 1958

Adapted from <http://time.com/4429096/black-lives-matter-civil-rights-photography/>. Accessed on May 16, 2019.

5 Now focus on the pictures and their captions. Then check the appropriate option to complete each sentence.

a Photojournalism articles...
  ☐ use pictures just to illustrate the news story and make the page look nice.
  ☐ combine pictures and narration to tell a news story.

b The captions...
  ☐ don't identify the people in the pictures, they only express the journalist's opinion.
  ☐ identify the people in place and time and present facts.

c The pictures...
  ☐ have meaning in context and help the readers make connections with the written text.
  ☐ have no connection with the text.

Post-reading

6 Talk to a partner about recent examples of similar uses of photography in the media.

89

L2

Toolbox Present simple x past simple x present perfect

1 Read the posters and answer the questions. Then discuss with your classmates.

Text 1

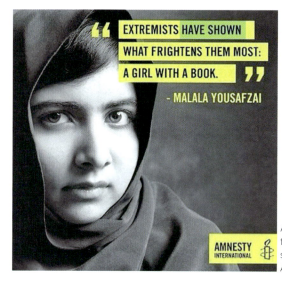

Adapted from <https://twitter.com/amnestyusa/status/785853829053022208>. Accessed on May 16, 2019.

Text 2

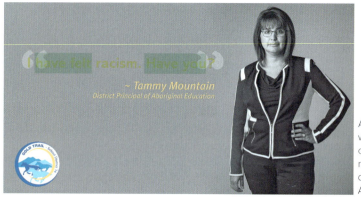

Adapted from <https://www.cbc.ca/news/canada/british-columbia/racism-campaign-school-district-74-1.4566779>. Accessed on May 16, 2019.

a Do you recognize the girl in the first poster? In your opinion, why would some people fear a girl with a book?

___

b Why do you think the woman in the second poster has suffered racism?

___

2 Now read these paragraphs and check your answers to activity 1.

At the end of 2008, the Taliban **prohibited** all female education. Malala **started** a blog for BBC Urdu, in which she **spoke up** for the girls' right to keep going to school. Because of her ideas, she **was** shot in the head on a bus on her way home from school in 2012.

Adapted from <https://www.bbc.com/news/magazine-24379018>. Accessed on May 12, 2019.

Tammy Mountain **directs** The Gold Trail School District in British Columbia, Canada, where 60% of the students **are** from indigenous communities.

Adapted from <http://www.sd74.bc.ca/District/abed/Pages/default.aspx>. Accessed on May 12, 2019.

3 Observe the highlighted verb forms in activities 1 and 2. Then complete the sentences with *present simple*, *present perfect* and *past simple*.

a The verbs highlighted in blue express facts in the present time, so they are in the _____.

b The verbs highlighted in yellow express events that happened in the past, so they are in the _____.

c The verbs highlighted in green refer to a fact that started in the past and has a consequence in the present (poster 1) or to life experiences (poster 2), so they are in the _____.

4 Read the excerpts from a book about racism in the United States and circle the appropriate options to complete the statements.

Text 1

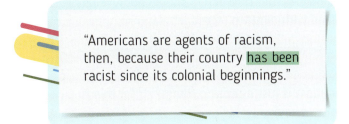

"Americans are agents of racism, then, because their country has been racist since its colonial beginnings."

Text 2

"We shop at stores that hire virtually no blacks. We send our children to schools that we know are better than those available to most blacks and other racial minorities."

FAIR, Bryan K. *Notes of a Racial Caste Baby:* **Color Blindness and the End of Affirmative Action.** New York; London: New York University Press, 1997. p. 63-64.

a In text 1, the highlighted verb form is in the **present perfect/present simple** tense, which is formed by subject + auxiliary verb (have/has) + main verb in the **infinitive/past participle**. "Been" is the past participle of the verb to be and indicates that the event started in the past and continues in the present.

b In text 2, the highlighted verbs are in the **present perfect/present simple** tense. They express present facts and routines. If "we" was replaced by "he" or "she", the conjugation of the highlighted verbs would be **shops/shopped**, **sends/sent** and **knows/known**.

5 Now read these sentences and answer the questions.

I Tammy Mountain does not direct a school in England.

II The Taliban did not prohibit male education.

III Extremists have not shown respect for human life.

a Which auxiliary verbs are used to form the negative?

_____

b In which sentence the main verb is not in the infinitive form? What is the verb tense used?

_____

c If you want to ask a question in the present simple, past simple or present perfect, where do you place the auxiliary verb: before or after the subject?

_____

L2

Building blocks — Connectors (linking words)

1 Read these excerpts from the book *The Diary of a Young Girl*, by Anne Frank. Then match them to the corresponding topics.

a "'This is the beginning of the end,' everyone was saying, **but** Churchill, the British Prime Minister, [...] declared, [...] 'It is not even the beginning of the end'. [...] **However**, there's reason for optimism. Stalingrad [...] still hasn't fallen into German hands." (p. 50)

b "You mustn't get the idea that he's starving. We found bread, cheese, jam **and** eggs in his cupboard. It's absolutely disgraceful that Dussel [...] should not give us anything. **After all**, we've shared all we had with him!" (p. 77)

c "I have only one hope: that this anti-Semitism is just a passing thing, [...] **for** this is unjust!" (p. 224)

d "Women should be respected **as well**! Generally speaking, men are held in great esteem in all parts of the world, **so** why shouldn't women have their share?" (p. 235)

FRANK, Anne. *The Diary of a Young Girl.* New York: Doubleday, 1995.

☐ prejudice ☐ lack of resources ☐ war ☐ sexism

> **Going further**
> *The Diary of a Young Girl* is a book based on the diary written by Anne Frank, a teenage Jewish girl who had to live hidden for two years during the Nazi occupation in the Netherlands.

2 Complete this list with the connectors highlighted in activity 1 according to what they express.

a	addition	too,
b	conclusion	all in all,
c	contrast	though,
d	effect or result	therefore,
e	reason	because,

3 Use the connectors from activities 1 and 2 to complete these extracts from Anne Frank's biography.

a In 1939, Germany invaded Poland. Would they invade the Netherlands _____? Anne's father considered moving to another place, _____ decided to stay.

b The Franks had to be careful not to be caught by the Nazis. _____ they covered all the windows with thick curtains.

c Anne and her family believed that the war was coming to an end. _____, on August 4, 1944, the Nazis stormed into the Franks' hideout _____ took everyone captive.

d Anne liked to read _____ dreamed of being a writer someday. Despite her sad story, she became a famous writer indeed. _____, her diary was published in over sixty-five different languages.

Adapted from <https://www.ducksters.com/biography/women_leaders/anne_frank.php>. Accessed on May 20, 2019.

4 Now read these extracts from the text in the "Explore" section. Then check the appropriate options.

"**Because of this**, activists looked for the type of photographic coverage that **not only** showed the intensity of the struggle, **but also** made the massive resistance to change visible."
"These pictures represent only a millisecond of a long, contested struggle. **Yet**, as they are shared and broadcast online, they shape how we see and remember these events for years to come."

a In the extracts, "because of this", "not only… but also…" and "yet" express _____, respectively.

☐ addition, contrast and reason   ☐ reason, addition and contrast

b Which of these connectors express addition?

☐ "and", "as well (as)", "not only… but also", "too"   ☐ "and", "all in all", "too"

c To express reason, it is possible to use…

☐ "for", "so" and "because of this".   ☐ "because", "for" and "because of this".

d If you want to contrast ideas, you can use…

☐ "but", "however", "though" and "yet".   ☐ "all in all", "but", "though" and "yet".

5 Now go back to the excerpts in activity 1 and discuss these questions with a partner.

a Have you seen in the news recently any situation in which people lack resources? Tell your partner about it.

b In the last excerpt, Anne Frank says that women were not respected at that time. Can you think of examples of women being disrespected nowadays? Do you think things have changed? Why?

L3

Sync Listening: Give nothing to racism

Pre-listening

1. Read this text from a campaign against discrimination. Then circle the appropriate options to complete the sentences.

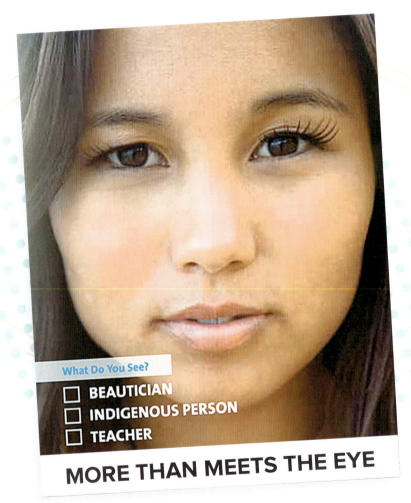

Adapted from <https://www.un.org/en/letsfightracism/>. Accessed on May 16, 2019.

a. This campaign shows that there **is/isn't** prejudice against indigenous people.
b. The campaign reminds us that we **should/should not** judge people by their appearance.
c. The text in the campaign **intends/doesn't intend** to convince readers to rethink their attitudes.
d. The campaign **uses/doesn't use** persuasive elements such as word choice, a slogan, short text and emotional appeal.

2. In your opinion, would racism and prejudice still exist if we were all blind? Check.

☐ No. Because we would not be able to discriminate people by the color of their skin, for example.

☐ Yes. We would use other aspects like the tone of voice and accent to form prejudiced stereotypes against people.

Listening

3 🎧14 **Listen to some visual-impaired people who were asked if they were racist. Then check the true statements.**

a ☐ All respondents think they are racist.
b ☐ Speakers 1 and 5 say that there are other ways to differentiate people's race besides looking at their skin color.
c ☐ Speaker 2 is curious about people's skin color.
d ☐ Speaker 3 says that if a person has no distinctive accent, he can't tell the person's race.
e ☐ Speaker 4 thinks that she can't be racist because she is blind.

4 🎧14 **Listen again and take notes to complete this chart.**

	Are you racist: yes or no?	Main ideias in the arguments
Speaker 1		Every _____ person is racist because capitalism was built on _____ and _____. _____ is not the only way to differentiate people's culture or race.
Speaker 2		Blind people don't usually ask about people's _____.
Speaker 3		It's impossible to know someone's race if you can't tell by his or her _____ or _____.
Speaker 4		She can't _____.
Speaker 5		Stereotypes: if people use slang or vulgar language, he thinks that they are _____.

Post-listening

5 **Discuss these questions with your classmates.**

a In your opinion, are campaigns like the one in activity 1 important to stop prejudice? Explain.
b Do the visually-impaired people you listened to in activities 3 and 4 have different opinions about how they react towards racism? Based on their opinions, can you say whether racism is only related to what we see?

95

L3

Sync Speaking: Discussing human rights

Pre-speaking

1 Get into groups. List some human rights. If necessary, do some research and take notes. Choose one human right to investigate.

2 Look for photojournalism articles that focus on the human right you researched. Choose one article to talk about.

3 Think about how the article and the accompanying pictures represent that human right.

4 Go over this chapter and look for vocabulary and linking words to connect your ideas. If necessary, review the verbs in the past in the "Toolbox" section. Take notes.

5 Make sure to use examples of facts and experiences to make your point. Consider getting figures, graphs, interviews and other information to support your arguments.

Speaking

6 Now you are going to discuss the article with your group. Follow the instructions.

  a Present your arguments using the language you have learned.

  b Listen to your classmates' arguments and, if necessary, take notes on their opinions so you can discuss them later.

  c Make sure you and your classmates are polite and respectful during the discussion. Remember: you are debating ideas and people can have different points of view.

  d Try to come to a consensus on the topic.

> **Useful language**
> I believe…
> In my opinion, …
> Based on…
> I agree because…
> I'm sorry, but I have to disagree with you because…

Post-speaking

7 Discuss these questions with your classmates.

  a In your opinion, was the discussion polite and respectful? Why?

  b Do you think the discussion was useful for you to learn more about human rights and to defend and promote them? Why?

  c What did you learn from the discussion?

Studio: Campaign on people's rights

What: an awareness campaign to fight for people's rights
To whom: school; community
Media: paper; digital
Objective: change people's perception about an issue/problem

1. Get into groups and choose a right that you think has been disrespected recently in your community/city (a consumer right, a taxpayer right, an elderly person's right, an indigenous people's right etc.). Find more information about it.

2. Review the chapter for vocabulary you can use to prepare a poster campaign to alert your audience about the problem and persuade them to change it.

3. Decide on the strategies to persuade people to join the campaign.

4. Write the text for your poster. Think of how you can encourage your audience to reflect on the issue. Use a bilingual dictionary to help you if necessary.

5. Choose pictures to use in your poster. Make sure they help you make your point and cause an impact on the audience. Combine text and pictures.

6. Review your text to see whether the ideas are clear and the arguments are logical to make the audience reflect on the issue and be persuaded to change. Make any necessary adjustments.

7. Show the material to other groups and ask them for feedback on how to improve it. Make comments on their material too. Then make changes if necessary.

8. As a class, decide where to display the posters. Check if you are allowed to hang posters in your chosen places and display them.

9. Analyze the other groups' posters. Do they make you reflect? Are you disrespecting any right in your community/city? How could you change it?

10. Publish your work on the **Students for PEACE Social Media** <www.studentsforpeace.com.br>, using the tag **awarenesscampaign** or others chosen by the students.

8 Freedom of speech

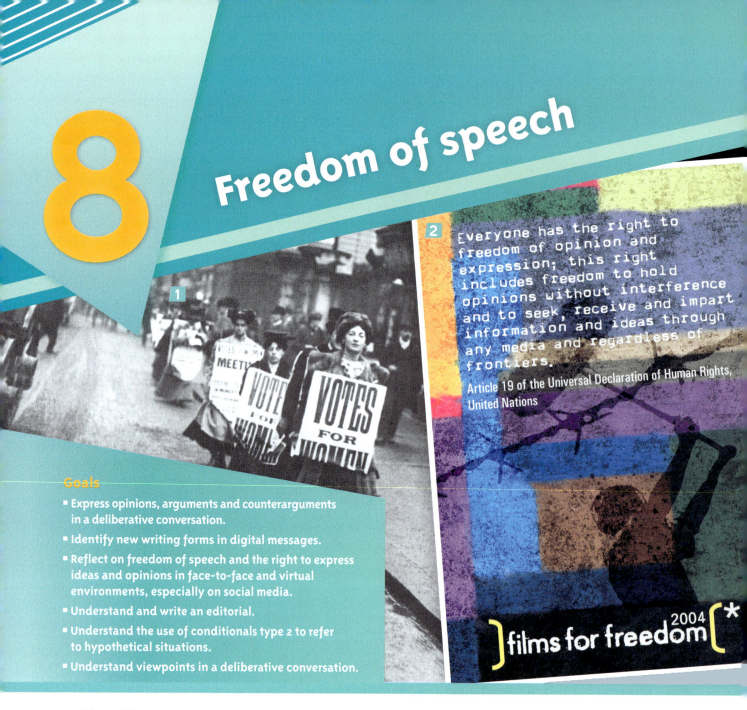

Goals

- Express opinions, arguments and counterarguments in a deliberative conversation.
- Identify new writing forms in digital messages.
- Reflect on freedom of speech and the right to express ideas and opinions in face-to-face and virtual environments, especially on social media.
- Understand and write an editorial.
- Understand the use of conditionals type 2 to refer to hypothetical situations.
- Understand viewpoints in a deliberative conversation.

Spark

1 Look at the pictures and number the descriptions accordingly.

a ☐ A poster with Article 19 of the Universal Declaration of Human Rights, proclaimed by the United Nations General Assembly in Paris on December 10, 1948.

b ☐ A poster for the World Day Against Cyber Censorship campaign, promoted by Amnesty International in 2016, with chinese activist Ai Weiwei.

c ☐ A wall graffiti representing freedom of speech in the Borough of Tower Hamlets, an area renowned for its street art in East London, England.

d ☐ Suffragettes demonstrate in favor of votes for women in London, 1912.

e ☐ People cover their mouths to protest against censorship and prohibition of freedom of speech in Krakow, Poland, 2018.

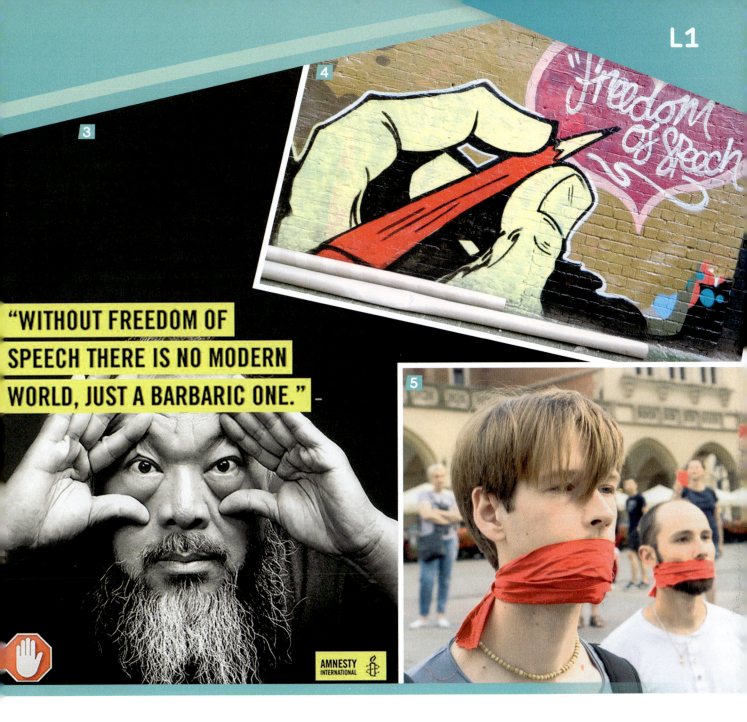

2. Answer these questions. Then discuss with your classmates.

a In your opinion, which of the five pictures best represents the topic of this chapter? Why?

b Have you seen similar protests, campaigns or events in your community, in your city or somewhere else in Brazil recently? If so, what were they about?

c In your opinion, how can we respectfully exercise the right to free speech online?

L1

Pre-reading

1 Read this extract from a Canadian online newspaper and complete the tasks.

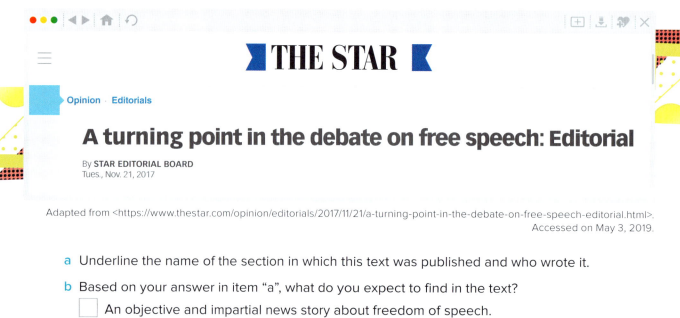

Adapted from <https://www.thestar.com/opinion/editorials/2017/11/21/a-turning-point-in-the-debate-on-free-speech-editorial.html>. Accessed on May 3, 2019.

a Underline the name of the section in which this text was published and who wrote it.

b Based on your answer in item "a", what do you expect to find in the text?
- [ ] An objective and impartial news story about freedom of speech.
- [ ] The newspaper's opinion on a news story about freedom of speech.

Reading

2 Read the introduction to the editorial. Then write *T* (true) or *F* (false).

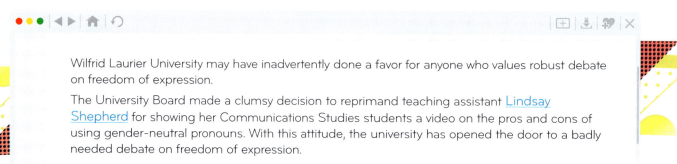

Adapted from <https://www.thestar.com/opinion/editorials/2017/11/21/a-turning-point-in-the-debate-on-free-speech-editorial.html>. Accessed on May 3, 2019.

a ☐ The editorial expresses the newspaper's opinion about a news story involving Wilfrid Laurier University and Lindsay Shepherd.

b ☐ Wilfrid Laurier University wanted to start a debate on freedom of expression.

c ☐ Wilfrid Laurier University approved of Lindsay Shepherd's action.

d ☐ The newspaper board believes it is extremely necessary to debate freedom of expression.

L1

3. **Read the continuation of the editorial and circle the appropriate option to complete each statement.**

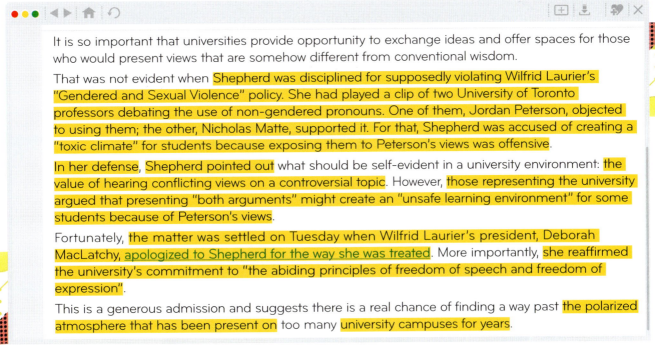

It is so important that universities provide opportunity to exchange ideas and offer spaces for those who would present views that are somehow different from conventional wisdom.

That was not evident when Shepherd was disciplined for supposedly violating Wilfrid Laurier's "Gendered and Sexual Violence" policy. She had played a clip of two University of Toronto professors debating the use of non-gendered pronouns. One of them, Jordan Peterson, objected to using them; the other, Nicholas Matte, supported it. For that, Shepherd was accused of creating a "toxic climate" for students because exposing them to Peterson's views was offensive.

In her defense, Shepherd pointed out what should be self-evident in a university environment: the value of hearing conflicting views on a controversial topic. However, those representing the university argued that presenting "both arguments" might create an "unsafe learning environment" for some students because of Peterson's views.

Fortunately, the matter was settled on Tuesday when Wilfrid Laurier's president, Deborah MacLatchy, apologized to Shepherd for the way she was treated. More importantly, she reaffirmed the university's commitment to "the abiding principles of freedom of speech and freedom of expression".

This is a generous admission and suggests there is a real chance of finding a way past the polarized atmosphere that has been present on too many university campuses for years.

Adapted from <https://www.thestar.com/opinion/editorials/2017/11/21/a-turning-point-in-the-debate-on-free-speech-editorial.html>. Accessed on May 3, 2019.

a. The authors believe universities **must/must not** allow people to express different ideas.

b. Lindsay Shepherd exposed her students to **academic/non-academic** opinions about the use of non-gendered pronouns.

c. One of these opinions **was interpreted/was not interpreted** as offensive.

d. The right to speak one's mind is a difficult issue **only on Wilfrid Laurier University campus/in many university campuses**.

4. **Read the text in activity 3 again and check the options that are appropriate.**

a. The highlighted excerpts in the text express…
   - [ ] facts (what happened).
   - [ ] opinions (what the authors think about the case).

b. The editorial mentions facts in order to provide…
   - [ ] a summary of the case and evidence that supports the authors' view.
   - [ ] a neutral position on the subject.

c. The main argument of the editorial consists of expressing that…
   - [ ] things have finally changed for those who speak their minds on university campuses.
   - [ ] universities must engage in serious debate on free speech.

Post-reading

5. **How do you usually react when someone disagrees with your views? Discuss with your classmates.**

Listen to:
Freedom of speech

L2

Toolbox Conditional sentences – type 2

1 Read this news extract and circle the appropriate option to complete its summary.

Web censorship: the net is closing in

Across the globe, governments are monitoring and censoring access to the web. And if we're not careful, one day millions of people will find the internet fractured, fragmented and controlled by the state.

▲ Customers at an internet cafe in Guilin, China, where the government places severe restrictions on web access.

Photograph: Martin Puddy/Martin Puddy/Corbis

Adapted from *The Guardian*, London, April 23, 2013.

This piece of news is about the restriction imposed by governments on freedom **in internet cafes**/**on the internet**.

2 Read these extracts about free speech. What's your opinion about them?

a "Users would have to agree to certain conditions to access a country's internet. So, if your IP address came from an untrustworthy country, you would encounter higher monitoring."

Adapted from *The Guardian*, London, April 23, 2013.

b "If a government succeeded in creating an alternative internet system, it could effectively unplug its population from the global internet and instead offer them only a closed, national intranet."

Adapted from *The Guardian*, London, April 23, 2013.

c "We protect speech because of its effects. If speech had no effects, it wouldn't be a fundamental right."

The New York Times, New York, September 13, 2017.

d "Wouldn't that be great if life were so easy? Unfortunately, there is no such thing as a legal line between free speech and hate speech."

Adapted from <https://www.quora.com/How-do-you-differentiate-between-hate-speech-and-free-speech>. Accessed on April 10, 2019.

3 Based on the extracts in activity 2, complete the paragraph with the words from the box.

> blue   two   yellow

There are _____ highlighted clauses in each item. The clauses in _____ introduce imaginary conditions and the clauses in _____ introduce possible, but also imaginary, results of such conditions.

4 Study the extracts in activity 2 again and check the appropriate options.

a In the same way as in zero and in first conditional (types 0 and 1), "if" is a conjunction that introduces…

- [ ] conditions.
- [ ] results.

b Clauses that introduce imaginary present or future conditions contain…

- [ ] a verb in the past tense (affirmative or negative).
- [ ] "would" (or "could") + verb in the infinitive form (affirmative, negative or interrogative).

c Clauses that express a possible imaginary result contain…

- [ ] a verb in the past tense (affirmative or negative).
- [ ] "would" (or "could") + verb in the infinitive form (affirmative, negative or interrogative).

d The negative is formed by adding "not"…

- [ ] after "would" and "could".
- [ ] before "would" and "could".

> **Going further**
>
> The sentence in item "d" from activity 2 says: "*Wouldn't that be great if life **were** so easy?*". The construction with **were** is possible only in second conditional sentences: *if I were* (or *if I was*), *if he/she/it were* (or *if he/she/it was*). *Were* is most commonly used in more formal contexts, but both forms are possible.

5 Complete these questions with the appropriate form of the verbs in the box. Then ask and answer the questions with a partner.

> make   restrict   say

a What would you do if a friend _____ something horrible about your favorite band?

b What would you do if someone _____ a negative comment about something you posted online?

c What would you miss most if the government of your country _____ the access to all social media websites and apps?

L2

Building blocks — Internet language

1 Answer the questions. Then discuss with your classmates.

a How often do you communicate virtually with people through writing?

b What apps or social media tools do you usually use for communication? If you don't use any, which one/s do you know?

c Do you write messages online using the same language as when you write messages on paper? Why?

2 Match the three resources to their definitions.

a abbreviation   b emoji   c pseudo-acronym

☐ A sequence of numbers and/or letters that represents longer words with fewer characters.

☐ A small digital picture or icon used to express an idea or emotion.

☐ A shortened form of a word or phrase that represents the full form.

3 Read and match each post from a microblogging website to its central message/purpose.

_____ To agree with and congratulate someone on his/her attitude towards freedom of speech.

_____ To disagree with the person who complained about the profile's content and to claim we have free speech.

Text 1

Emma Stewart
@qcEmmaStewart
Follow

Replying to @ScanBC

This is not a government site. If u don't like it, ur free to unfollow. We have free speech & u don't decide 4us.

Text 2

Elton Yamamoto
@MrYamamoto
Follow

It is impressive that a mainstream artist like @newStar is taking this transparent & progressive stand on freedom of expression. #CreditWhereDue 👏👏

4 Complete these sentences with examples of internet language/resources from the posts in activity 3.

a Abbreviations: _____ in place of "you", _____ in place of "you are" and _____ in place of "and".

b Emoji: _____ to express approval or appreciation of someone else's post.

c Pseudo-acronym: _____ in place of "for us".

5 Match these common abbreviations and pseudo-acronyms often used in text messages to their meanings.

a	ab	☐	in my opinion
b	bc	☐	about
c	b4	☐	to be honest
d	BTW	☐	whatever
e	brb	☐	before
f	F2F	☐	face to face
g	LOL	☐	I don't know
h	OFC	☐	of course
i	imo	☐	by the way
j	idk	☐	be right back
k	TBH	☐	because
l	wtv	☐	laughing out loud

6 Let's play a guessing game! Draw five emojis or emoticons and challenge your classmates to guess what they mean.

L3

Sync Listening: Expressing opinions and reaching a consensus

Pre-listening

1 Read this excerpt from a newspaper editorial. Then answer the questions.

USA TODAY, November 18, 2015

Campus adults, protect free speech: our view

The Editorial Board, USA TODAY.

When student protests and the resignation of the university president revealed deep racial problems at the University of Missouri last week, it seemed at first like a singular event.

Since then, it's become increasingly clear that similar tensions are raging on campuses from Connecticut to California.

Adapted from <https://www.usatoday.com/story/opinion/2015/11/18/campus-speech-yale-missouri-race-freedom-editorials-debates/76005634/>. Accessed on June 4, 2019.

a What is the title of the text? Who wrote it?

b Is it an opinion text? Explain your answer.

Listening

2 🎧 15 Listen to the opening of the Editorial Board meeting shown in activity 1. Order the topics the editor mentions.

a ☐ Racism on campus.
b ☐ Pushing out administrators.
c ☐ The power of the college football teams.
d ☐ The limits of free speech on campus.

3 🎧 16 **Listen to the next part of the meeting. Then circle the appropriate option/s to complete the sentences.**

a The speakers are discussing topics number **1/2/3/4** from activity 2.

b The speakers have **the same/different** points of view on the topics.

4 🎧 16 **Listen to the audio again. Write the number of the speaker next to the argument he/she defends.**

a Speaker ☐ : A black gay man is student body president, so Mizzou can't be considered racist.

b Speaker ☐ : Universities should teach a class on the First Amendment and free speech. People might not feel that they have the right to say what they want if they are fired for it.

c Speaker ☐ : Mizzou has systemic racism built within the college structure and its president doesn't know how to deal with race.

d Speaker ☐ : Tim Wolf is not a good president, but this has nothing to do with the First Amendment issue on campus.

> **Going further**
>
> This is the First Amendment to the United States Constitution:
>
> *"Congress shall make no law respecting an establishment of religion, or prohibiting the free exercise thereof; or abridging the freedom of speech, or of the press; or the right of the people peaceably to assemble, and to petition the Government for a redress of grievances."*
>
> McWHIRTER, Robert J. *The First Amendment:* **An Illustrated History.** Tempe: Constitution Press, 2017. p. 3.
>
> Is there a similar law in Brazil? Do some research and share the results with your classmates.

Post-listening

5 **Discuss these questions with your classmates and check.**

a Was the debate you listened to respectful?

☐ Yes. Nobody used bad words or offended anybody. They focused on the facts and didn't mix them with personal situations.

☐ No. Everybody talked at the same time and they were rude to one another.

b How would you feel if you were in a similar debate?

☐ Comfortable. I like to express my opinions, argue and make counterarguments.

☐ Uncomfortable. I don't like to express my opinions, argue or make counterarguments.

L3

Sync Speaking: **A deliberative conversation**

Pre-speaking

 1 Let's prepare a deliberative conversation. Follow the instructions.

a Get into groups. Choose a topic that has been in the media recently. Consider a topic that requires suggestions of measures that can be taken to improve a situation or solve a problem.

b Find out more about it (e.g.: facts, what people have said about it etc.).

c Think about it and decide what your point of view is.

d Prepare the script. Refer to the "Useful language" box below. If necessary, use the dictionary or ask your teacher/classmates to help with the vocabulary you do not know.

e Practice expressing your views to members of different groups and listen to them as well.

f Give feedback to your classmates (if the arguments are persuasive, if the solutions are viable etc.) and listen to their feedback about your arguments. Make changes if necessary.

Useful language

Asking for opinion	Expressing opinion	Filler words	Agreeing	Disagreeing	Conceding
What do you think...?	One conclusion I've come to is that...	I mean...	I agree with you that...	But again...	If... was just about..., then I would agree with you.
Is everybody on board with...?	There are a few facts that we have to consider...	Right...	Fair enough.	I understand your point, but...	As long as...
	I think...	You know...	You've earned a point.	That's true, but...	
	It's about...		You have a point there.		

Speaking

 2 You are going to engage in a deliberative conversation.

a Get together with the members of your group. Decide who is going to be the mediator.

b In turns, express your views and say if you agree or disagree with your classmates' views.

c At the end, the mediator will summarize the opinions and check if everybody agrees with the results or solutions obtained in the deliberative conversation.

Post-speaking

 3 What have you learned from this activity? How was it to deal with different opinions? Did you take care not to sound rude when giving your opinion? Discuss.

> **What:** an editorial
> **To whom:** other students; people in general
> **Media:** paper; digital
> **Objective:** present an opinion about an issue that is relevant to your community

1. In groups, list some controversial news stories that have been grabbing your community's attention and choose one to investigate. Collect facts and opinions about it.

2. Decide on your position: whose views are you going to support? Why?

3. Choose the information to set the context for your editorial and to help you build your arguments. Organize the information you have collected according to viewpoints.

4. Choose some quotations that offer evidence to defend your opinion.

5. Review the characteristics of editorials in the "Explore" section and write the first draft of your text. Tips:
   - In the first paragraph, summarize the topics and state your opinion briefly.
   - Next, explain each opposing viewpoint with facts and quotations.
   - Refute the opposing views and express your opinion based on facts, figures, quotations etc.
   - If possible, suggest solutions.
   - Write a conclusion that restates the viewpoint expressed in the introduction.

6. Share your draft with other groups. Give and receive feedback. Make changes, if necessary, and finish your text.

7. Pin the final version of your editorial up on the classroom board for your classmates to read.

8. Discuss the editorials and the suggestions provided by each of them. Can these suggestions be put into practice?

9. Publish your work on the **Students for PEACE Social Media** <www.studentsforpeace.com.br>, using the tag **editorial** or others chosen by the students.

Peace talk

**Chapters 7 and 8
Agree to disagree**

1 There is a fine line between free speech and hate speech. You may be free to express yourself, but you should do it respectfully, without harming anyone. With this idea in mind, read the texts. Then answer the questions.

a What topic do texts 1 and 2 have in common? Explain your answer.

_____

_____

b How do you interpret the message in text 3? How is it different from the message in text 4?

_____

_____

2. "Agree to disagree" is the title of this section. What does this expression mean? Read these useful sentences to come up with an answer.

_____

_____

3. Do you ever use the "agree to disagree" skills to manage conflicts? In your opinion, how important is it to develop such skills in order to create a culture of peace? Discuss.

4. Read this statement made by one of South Africa's most well-known human rights activists. Then discuss the questions with a partner.

   a. Do you agree with Desmond Tutu? Explain your answer.

   b. How can we dialogue better? What can or cannot be said or done to defend an argument?

5. Have a round-table discussion practicing the "agree to disagree" skills. Follow the instructions.

   a. Choose a topic from the box to discuss. You can think of different topics as well.

   > being able to choose your school subjects   making your own food
   > using the smartphone in class   wearing uniforms to school

   b. Organize yourselves into two groups, one in favor of the topic and the other against it. Make a list of arguments to be used in order to defend your position.

   c. Ask the teacher or a student to mediate the debate. Start the round-table discussion.

   d. Use the appropriate linking words (connectors) whenever possible.

111

Self-assessment

Chapter 1 – The world of work

Can you understand graphs?

Can you talk about different careers?

Can you present the results of a survey orally?

Can you produce graphs to summarize information?

Chapter 2 – Tech in the world

Can you understand charts?

Can you talk about the positive and negative aspects of modern technology in our lives?

Can you present a mini-lesson based on visuals?

Can you produce charts and paragraphs to present data from a survey?

Chapter 3 – Citizenship

Can you understand forum posts?

Can you talk about citizenship and recognize the characteristics of a citizen?

Can you express your opinion about different types of government?

Can you write a forum post?

Chapter 4 – Sustainability

Can you understand the concept of "green attitudes"?

Can you understand and create an infographic about the environment and sustainability?

Can you mention some actions that contribute to the preservation of the planet?

Can you use the modals "should", "have to", "must", "may", "might" and "will" in sentences about the environment and sustainability?

Chapter 5 – Global and local

Can you understand opinion articles?

Can you talk about global and local issues?

Can you participate in a debate about global and local topics?

Can you write an opinion article?

Chapter 6 – Consumer society

Can you understand and define what consumerism is?

Can you understand the characteristics of an ad and produce one?

Can you ask and answer questions using the present perfect with "ever", "already", "yet" and "never"?

Can you use money and advertising vocabulary?

Chapter 7 – Fighting for our rights

Can you understand photojournalism articles and awareness campaigns?

Can you talk about the fight for human rights?

Can you participate in a discussion about an issue related to human rights, presenting arguments and considering different points of view?

Can you create a poster for an awareness campaign about people's rights?

Chapter 8 – Freedom of speech

Can you understand editorials?

Can you talk about freedom of speech?

Can you participate in deliberative conversations?

Can you write an editorial?

Workbook

Name: _____ Class: _____ Date: _____

Chapter 1 — The world of work

1 Read the graph and write *T* (true) or *F* (false).

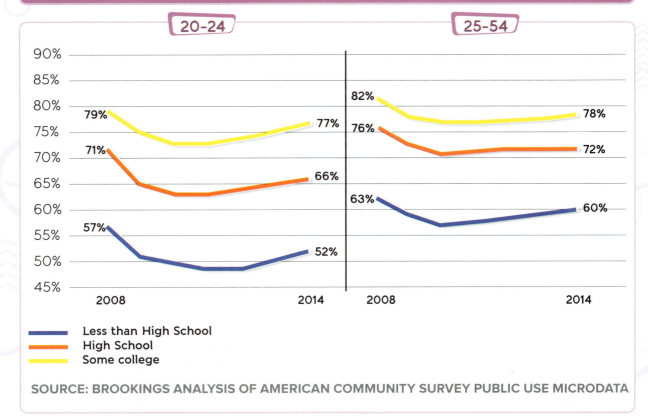

Adapted from <https://www.brookings.edu/research/employment-and-disconnection-among-teens-and-young-adults-the-role-of-place-race-and-education/>. Accessed on April 26, 2019.

a ☐ The graph does not show the employment rates among European young people.
b ☐ The graph presents data only about people who finished high school.
c ☐ The graph shows the employment situation in the United States between 2008 and 2014.
d ☐ The graph indicates that more people were working in 2008 than in 2014.

2 Circle the appropriate options based on the graph in activity 1.

a People who have not finished high school are in the group represented by the **red/blue** line.
b It is possible to infer that the number of people working in 2010-2011 was **lower/higher** than in 2008 in all cases.
c **More/Fewer** people with some college education were employed in 2008 compared to the other two categories.
d The graph **distinguishes/doesn't distinguish** between men and women.
e The information shown in the graph **is/is not** about a specific country.

3 Match the careers to their descriptions.

a Someone whose occupation is to give legal assistance to people.
b A person who can treat the diseases of the teeth and gums.
c A person whose job is to plan and build roads, bridges and similar structures.
d Someone who is employed to collect and dispose of garbage.
e A person whose occupation is to help people learn something.

☐ dentist ☐ lawyer ☐ sanitation worker ☐ teacher ☐ civil engineer

4 Complete the sentences with *will* or *going to* and the verbs in parentheses.

a By the year 2100, models predict sea level _____ (to rise) between 20 and 50 cm above late 20th century levels.
b Something tells me Jack _____ (to be) late for school again today.
c All the numbers show our team _____ (to win) the game tomorrow.
d Neil Anderson says 5G _____ (to take) longer to be implemented because many new microcell towers and base stations have to be built for this new technology.
e Why don't we go to the beach on Sunday? It _____ (to rain – neg.).

5 Read the text and check the appropriate options.

WE ASKED OUR AWESOME TEEN TWITTER FOLLOWERS TO SUMMARIZE THE SUMMER OF 2018 FOR US USING ONLY THREE WORDS. SEE THE MOST FREQUENT WORDS THEY SHARED VISUALIZED IN A WORD CLOUD.

YouTube, blogging, concerts, Twitter, study, rainy, internet, Bieber, BFF, friends, travel, baking, love, fantastic, sleep, food, fun, beach, music, busy, short, Demi, volleyball

Adapted from <https://www.huffpost.com/entry/1100-words-to-describe-your-summer00-words-to-describe-you_n_3853071>.
Accessed on April 27, 2019.

a The second most frequent word shows that, for many teenagers,
☐ vacations are too long.   ☐ vacations should be longer.

b Which words show that teenagers don't want to be alone on their summer vacation?
☐ Friends, BFF, volleyball.   ☐ Friends, sleep, fun.

c Which words tell us that teenagers like to be online during their vacation?
☐ YouTube, Twitter, blogging, internet.   ☐ Twitter, Bieber, Demi, internet.

Workbook

Name: _____ Class: _____ Date: _____

Chapter 2 Tech in the world

1 Read this text about technology and complete it with the missing sentences.

HOW MUCH DO YOU KNOW ABOUT TECHNOLOGY?

The internet is full of websites with curious information about technology. We have chosen some to present today. Here we go!

Did you know that approximately 6,000 new viruses are released every month? That is why specialists recommend that ☐.

Technology is everywhere, but ☐. Some people suffer from disorders like technophobia (the fear of technology), nomophobia (the fear of being without a mobile phone) or cyberphobia (the fear of computers). Can you imagine how hard it must be for them?

PCs, tablets and smartphones also affect the way your body works. For example, ☐. That is less than half of the normal rate of 20. This can lead to dry eyes and irritation.

Finally, did you know that November 30 is "Computer Security Day"? Specialists say that it's a good day to run some security checks and change your passwords because ☐.

Based on <https://globallead.co.za/2018/02/22/20-fun-facts-technology/>. Accessed on May 8, 2019.

a if you think everybody feels comfortable with it, you are completely wrong

b if you are an average computer user, you blink only seven times a minute

c PC users install reliable antivirus software if they want to be safe

d if you don't do this from time to time, your computer will be vulnerable

2 Read the text again and check the appropriate options.

a The aim of the text is to _____.
☐ inform the reader about technology
☐ persuade the reader to use technology

b The text is for _____.
☐ technology specialists
☐ people in general

c The text presents _____ about technology.
☐ facts
☐ personal opinions

d The content presented in the text mentions _____ aspects of technology.
☐ positive
☐ negative

115

3 Look at these technology-related words from the text. Then identify and underline the prefixes.

a antivirus
b cyberphobia
c internet
d technophobia

4 Use the prefixes in activity 3 to complete these questions.

a Do you ever read the _____ spam policy of the websites you sign up for?

b Is there a _____ cafe in your neighborhood?

c Do you use any _____ active programs to help you practice English?

d Do you know what "_____ culture" is? I guess we can say we live in one, given the amount of technology present in our daily lives.

5 Look at the pictures and complete the sentences with a clause that…

a expresses what generally happens or is true.

If you don't blink about 20 times a minute,

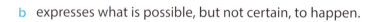.

b expresses what is possible, but not certain, to happen.

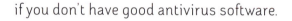

if you don't have good antivirus software.

c introduces a condition.

_____,

they will be able to download files much faster.

116

Workbook

Name: _____ Class: _____ Date: _____

Chapter 3 Citizenship

1 Read the text and write *T* (true) or *F* (false).

Who will be there for us when we grow old?

Old age does not have to be a bad thing. In some societies, the elderly are respected and admired. In India, for example, youngsters touch the feet of their elders as a "mark of love" and respect, and to request their blessings. In East Asia, children grow up knowing that they will have to exchange roles with their parents and care for them when they grow old. In China, however, adult children seem to have abandoned their elderly. The situation is so extreme that the government had to pass a law ordering adult children to visit their ageing parents.

According to the Elderly Rights Law, Chinese adults must find time to visit their parents "often". The law does not state when children should see their parents, but if someone disobeys, he/she has to pay a fine and may be sent to jail. The law also reminds citizens of the importance of respect, as it states that adults should not insult elderly people. In Brazil, there is no law obligating adult children to visit their parents if they don't want to, but they should at least respect the *Estatuto do Idoso*.

Based on <https://www.bbc.com/news/world-asia-china-23124345>; <https://www.marieclaire.co.uk/life/how-different-countries-treat-the-elderly-20839>. Accessed on April 12, 2019.

a ☐ Adults show respect for the elderly in India.
b ☐ In East Asia, adult children have no obligation to look after their parents.
c ☐ In China, the government forces adult children to visit their parents.
d ☐ There are no consequences if you break the Elderly Rights Law in China.
e ☐ In Brazil, there is a document that protects the rights of the elderly.

2 Match these extracts from the text in activity **1** to what they express.

a obligation
b no necessity
c recommendation

☐ "Old age does not have to be a bad thing"
☐ "they will have to exchange roles with their parents"
☐ "Chinese adults must find time to visit their parents 'often'"
☐ "children should see their parents"
☐ "he/she has to pay a fine"
☐ "adults should not insult elderly people"
☐ "they should at least respect the *Estatuto do Idoso*"

3 Fill in the blanks with *must*, *have to* or *should*. Keep the meaning of the original sentences.

I have the obligation to look after my pet.
I _____**must/have to**_____ look after my pet.

a Rick's room is a mess! It's a good idea to clean it.
Rick _____ clean his room.

b Citizens have the obligation to respect traffic laws.
Citizens _____ respect traffic laws.

c If you are an elderly person, it is not necessary to pay to ride the bus.
Elderly people _____ pay to ride the bus.

4 Complete these questions about citizenship with the words from the box.

distractedly   in need   pirated   priority   traffic

a What are the _____ laws in Brazil like? Can you give one example?

b What is the problem with buying _____ products?

c What can happen if you cross the road _____?

d How could you help people _____ in your community?

e Why must we respect _____ seating?

5 Choose three questions from activity 4 and answer them.

118

Workbook

Name: _____ Class: _____ Date: _____

Chapter 4 Sustainability

1 Read the infographic.

TOGETHER, WE CAN MAKE A DIFFERENCE

Small **changes** in behavior can have a **big impact** on our planet! When you *throw* something away, **where does it go**?

In the United States in 2015,

262.4 million tons of trash

were generated.

137.7 million tons ended up in landfills.

But it **doesn't** have to.

You can dramatically reduce the amount of trash that is thrown away by **taking a few easy steps**:

Reduce the amount of materials you use, which **reduces** the amount of waste you create.

Reuse materials.

Recycle whenever possible. **Rethink** the materials you use and those you **throw away**.

By **thinking about what we're using** and how to reduce the waste we produce, we can help **create a cleaner, healthier environment**.

Did you know?

About **76%** of food

that could be **composted**

ended up in **landfills**.

THE IMPACT

Recycling helps to create **cleaner land, air** and **water** and **better health**. Recycling and composting helps **save natural resources**.

Make a **difference today!**

If we take **small steps every day** to reduce the amount of waste we produce, **we can help protect the planet** for generations to come. For more information, visit www.epa.gov/recycle.

How **you** can help

In **stores**:

- Shop for products **made with recycled materials**.
- Buy items with **less packaging**.
- Buy refillable, **reusable containers**.
- Bring **your own bags to the store**.
- Buy only **what you need** or **what you know you will use** (applies to food as well).

At **home**:

- Use bags that you **already have** in your home and **recycle bags** that you no longer need if they can be recycled.
- Ask to **be removed from paper mailing lists**.
- Don't throw away anything that can be **reused or repaired**.
- For unwanted used electronics, **try upgrading the device to continue using it**. Otherwise, **donate or recycle it**.
- **Print on both sides of paper** (and use recycled paper) or do not print at all.
- **Compost** your food scraps or yard waste.

Based on *Advancing Sustainable Materials Management:* **Facts and Figures**, 2015.

2 Answer the questions about the infographic in activity 1.

a How many tons of trash were generated in the United States in 2015?

_____

b How many tons of trash ended up in landfills in the United States in 2015?

_____

3 Read the infographic in activity 1 again and check the appropriate options.

a According to the text, small actions…
- [ ] can be meaningful and help the planet.
- [ ] are important, but cannot help much.

b The text suggests that…
- [ ] it is impossible to reduce the amount of trash we throw away. We can only recycle the waste we create, not reduce it.
- [ ] it is possible to reduce the amount of trash we throw away by reducing the amount of materials we use and then reusing or recycling them.

4 Which of the measures recommended in activity 1 do you already do? What habits should you change? Complete the chart.

What I already do	Habits I should change

5 Read the sentences and circle the appropriate options according to the cues given.

a People **don't have to/mustn't** throw trash on the floor. They **should/must** use the trash cans provided. (prohibition; obligation)

b Governments **have to/should** promote sustainability. (necessity)

c People and supermarkets **shouldn't/mustn't** waste food. (recommendation)

d Ocean levels **will/may** rise in the next decades due to the melting of glaciers, which is a consequence of global warming. (probability – certain to happen)

e If the authorities don't take any action, more natural disasters **must/might** happen soon. (probability – not so certain to happen)

f Everybody **should/must** put the recyclable materials in the appropriate containers. (obligation)

120

Workbook

Name: _____ Class: _____ Date: _____

Chapter 5 Global and local

1 Read the article and find the information.

| AGENDA | INITIATIVES | REPORTS | EVENTS | ABOUT |

THIS IS WHAT COUNTRIES AROUND THE WORLD THINK ABOUT GLOBALIZATION

Written by Jeff Desjardins

Today's chart highlights data on the topic of globalization according to 12 countries. It is part of a survey that covers international trade, foreign direct investment and the impact of immigration. The first question was "Do you think globalization is a good or bad force for the world?"

COUNTRY	GOOD FORCE	BAD FORCE	DON'T KNOW
Australia	48%	22%	29%
Denmark	68%	15%	17%
Finland	56%	18%	27%
France	37%	37%	26%
Germany	60%	20%	20%
India	83%	7%	10%
Malaysia	73%	10%	17%
Sweden	63%	20%	18%
Thailand	76%	12%	12%
United Kingdom	46%	19%	36%
United States	40%	27%	33%
Vietnam	91%	4%	5%

Interestingly, support for globalization ranges from 37% (France) all the way to 91% (Vietnam), representing a very diverse array of attitudes towards the topic.

Adapted from <https://www.weforum.org/agenda/2017/11/what-your-country-thinks-of-globalization>.
Accessed on August 23, 2018.

a Where the article was published: _____

b Date of publication: _____

c The main topic of the article: _____

2 Write *T* (true) or *F* (false) according to the article.

a ☐ The article is about the author's opinion regarding globalization.

b ☐ No South American country is shown in the survey.

c ☐ The survey was published in 2017.

d ☐ Vietnam has the most negative opinion about globalization.

3 Complete this post about globalization using the words from the box. Then answer the question.

> In addition   In conclusion   For example   However

For most of human history, a person had limited access to other cultures. Now this has changed dramatically. Some people speak of cultural imperialism. _____, I see a positive side. _____, garage bands in Iceland can find an audience far beyond their island. _____, people can be free of restrictive mindsets as more and more ideas flow around. _____, I am excited about this new era.

Andre Lot

Adapted from <https://www.nytimes.com/2014/06/01/opinion/a-global-community.html>. Accessed on May 13, 2019.

Does this person think globalization is a positive or negative force?
_____

4 Complete the sentences using the present perfect of the verbs in parentheses.

a We _____ in Hong Kong. (live)
b Brazil _____ many products to Europe. (export)
c Sarah _____ at a multinational company. (work)
d You _____ at this school. (study)
e My friends _____ soccer. (play)

5 Rewrite the sentences in activity 4 adding *since* or *for* and the time expression given.

a five months: _____
b colonial times: _____
c ten years: _____
d you were a child: _____
e they started at the new school: _____

Workbook

Name: _____ Class: _____ Date: _____

Chapter 6 Consumer society

1 Look at this advertisement and complete the chart.

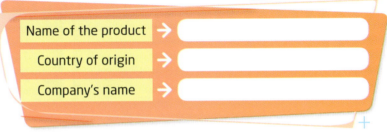

"Here's to another year – and years and years of Steady Nerves, Clear Brains and Vigorous Health"

Name of the product	→	
Country of origin	→	
Company's name	→	

Available at <https://www.viintage.com/album/vintage-public-domain-advertisements-and-ephemera-from-1911-1920-free/>. Accessed on May 30, 2019.

2 Read the advertisement again and check the false statement.

☐ The ad promoted a new product in the market at that time.

☐ The ad tries to convince the public that this product is good for their health.

3 Look at the pictures. Then make sentences using the cues given and *already*, *ever* or *yet*.

a
Marianna/clean her room

b
Paul/be to Olinda?

c
Mia and Anne/choose all the gifts

d
Bob/finish his work

123

4 Read the cues and complete the puzzle with words related to money.

DOWN

1. Samuel got a _____ from ABC shop for his birthday.
2. If you don't pay off your _____, the bank charges 5% interest per month.
3. Let's go to the ATM. I need to _____ some cash to pay this bill.
4. Peter wants to _____ money every month to buy a car.
5. Can you _____ me some cash to buy a sandwich, please?

ACROSS

6. You can pay for these shoes in four _____.
7. You shouldn't _____ your pocket money on silly things.
8. Can I _____ three dollars for the subway? I'll pay you back tomorrow.

Workbook

Name: _____ Class: _____ Date: _____

Chapter 7 Fighting for our rights

1 Complete the text about the Suffrage Movement using the connectors from the box.

| after all | and | because | however | so |

Women's fight for the right to vote in the UK

In the 19th century, many British men and women – including Queen Victoria – didn't believe that women should have the right to vote.

_____, many women thought differently, _____ they formed two main political groups: the National Union of Women's Suffrage Societies (NUWSS) and the Women's Social and Political Union (WSPU).

The two groups wanted basically the same: women's right to vote. They wore the colors purple, white and green; they organized marches and made banners with the words "Votes for Women" on them. But they used very different tactics.

Women in the former group campaigned for votes for middle-class, property-owning women _____ believed in peaceful protest. Women in the latter group welcomed women from all different walks of life, broke windows and went on hunger strikes to call public attention.

Their fight was hard. Some newspapers even invented the names *suffragist*, for the members of the NUWSS, and *suffragettes*, for the members of the WSPU, _____ they wanted to ridicule the movements.

Despite all the difficulties, the fight continued until World War I, a time that changed women's role in society. They had to work for the first time in different industries, _____, the men had been sent away to fight. As for the suffrage movements, they finally succeeded in 1928.

Based on <https://www.natgeokids.com/uk/discover/history/general-history/suffragettes-facts/>. Accessed on May 30, 2019.

2 Rewrite these extracts from the text in activity **1** replacing the connectors in bold, but keeping the same meaning.

a **However**, many women thought differently, **so** they formed two main political groups.

_____

b Some newspapers invented the names [...] **because** they wanted to ridicule the movements.

_____

c They had to work for the first time in different industries, **after all**, the men had been sent away to fight.

_____

125

3 Read the text in activity 1 again and write *T* (true) or *F* (false).

a ☐ All women wanted to vote in the UK in the 19th century.
b ☐ There were three principal groups for women's rights.
c ☐ There were similarities between the groups.
d ☐ One group was pacific and the other was more violent.
e ☐ The newspapers defended the women's cause.
f ☐ It was easy for women to be granted the right to vote.

4 Look at the text in activity 1 and find these examples of verbs in the past simple form.

a A verb in the negative form: _____

b Seven irregular verbs: _____

c Eleven regular verbs: _____

5 Read and complete the text with the verbs in parentheses in the present simple, present perfect or past simple forms.

Agewell Foundation is an NGO that _____ (work) for the welfare of the elderly of India since 1999. It usually _____ (launch) campaigns with posters that _____ (remind) us that it is really important to give attention to our elderly. Because of this, volunteers across India _____ (interact) with older people every day. They also _____ (help) by donating warm clothes during the winter. A lot of people _____ (benefit) from the winter campaign so far. In the 2017-2018 winter, for example, they _____ (collect) over 120,000 items of clothing and _____ (distribute) them amongst more than 80,000 elderly and destitute in Delhi-NCR.

Based on <https://www.agewellfoundation.org/?page_id=1230>; <https://www.agewellfoundation.org/>. Accessed on May 30, 2019.

Chapter 8 Freedom of speech

1 Read the text and write *T* (true) or *F* (false).

Emotikis bring indigenous culture to text messaging

By Danny Lewis Smithsonian.com

September 6, 2016

In recent years, there has been a push to include more diversity in emojis. For instance, adding new options for a variety of skin tones in smiley faces.

But when people from the Te Puia Maori cultural center in Rotorua, New Zealand, looked at existing emojis, they realized there was an opportunity to create some that reflected their country's indigenous cultures. Now there are more than 150 emojis. They have been dubbed "Emotikis". The pictograms include traditional objects from Maori culture, such as outrigger canoes, a traditional weapon called a "*taiaha*", and a "*tiki*" making all kinds of faces.

"We see these as a lighthearted and inclusive way to share the meaning of Maori words and concepts with other cultures and with all New Zealanders," said Te Puia spokesperson Kiri Atkinson-Crean.

Although the emojis were designed to be fun, the creators believe the Emotikis also give Maori youth more freedom to express themselves. Before the Emotikis, indigenous people could only use expressions and symbols from other countries when they engaged with each other online. Now they will be able to use technology that is inclusive and has signifiers from their own culture.

The Emotiki app will be available for download for free on smartphones and tablets.

Adapted from <https://www.tweentribune.com/article/tween56/emotikis-and-new-keyboards-bring-indigenous-culture-text-messaging/>. Accessed on May 15, 2019.

☐ Emojis are more inclusive now than in the past.
☐ The existing emojis were enough to reflect the indigenous culture.
☐ The use of Emotikis is not restricted to Maori people.
☐ The Maori can use Emotikis to refer to things that exist in their culture.
☐ You have to pay to use Emotikis on your smartphone.

127

2 Look at the picture that illustrates the text in activity 1. What does it show?

☐ Outrigger canoes. ☐ A "*tiki*" making all kinds of faces.
☐ A traditional weapon called a "*taiaha*".

3 Read these comments from an online forum about Emotikis. What do the pseudo-acronyms mean?

Paul: Check this article about Emotikis. Any opinions?
Manny: (a) **OFC** I'm gonna use them! (b) **BTW**, where can I download the app?
Sarah: (c) **idk**, have u tried the app store?
Jack: (d) **TBH**, I didn't like it.
Prince: (e) **imo**, it's a lot of fun!

a _____   d _____
b _____   e _____
c _____

4 Are there any abbreviations in the text in activity 3? If so, which one(s)?

_____

5 Now write a paragraph expressing your opinion about the news in activity 1 and the comments in activity 3.

_____
_____

6 Complete these clauses using the appropriate form of the verbs from the box. Then finish the sentences with information about yourself.

have   lose   meet   wake up

a If I _____ only 24 hours to live, _____.

b If I _____ my favorite singer, _____.

c If I _____ rich one morning, _____.

d If I _____ my smartphone with lots of important information on it, _____.

Irregular verbs list

Infinitive	Past simple	Past participle	Translation
be	was/were	been	*estar; ser*
become	became	become	*tornar(-se)*
bring	brought	brought	*trazer*
build	built	built	*construir*
catch	caught	caught	*pegar*
cut	cut	cut	*cortar*
do	did	done	*fazer*
drink	drank	drunk	*beber*
fall	fell	fallen	*cair*
feel	felt	felt	*sentir*
find	found	found	*achar, encontrar*
forbid	forbade	forbidden	*proibir*
forget	forgot	forgotten	*esquecer*
get	got	got/gotten	*chegar; ficar; obter*
give	gave	given	*dar*
go	went	gone	*ir*
have	had	had	*ter*
hide	hid	hidden	*esconder, ocultar*
keep	kept	kept	*guardar; manter*
know	knew	known	*conhecer; saber*
leave	left	left	*deixar; partir*
let	let	let	*deixar, permitir*
lose	lost	lost	*perder*
make	made	made	*fazer; preparar*
meet	met	met	*encontrar(-se)*
overcome	overcame	overcome	*superar; vencer*
put	put	put	*por; colocar*
ride	rode	ridden	*andar (a cavalo, de bicicleta, de moto etc.)*
run	ran	run	*correr*
say	said	said	*dizer*
see	saw	seen	*ver*
send	sent	sent	*enviar*
speak	spoke	spoken	*falar*
spend	spent	spent	*gastar*
take	took	taken	*aceitar; levar; pegar; tomar*
teach	taught	taught	*ensinar*
tell	told	told	*contar, dizer*
think	thought	thought	*achar; pensar*
throw	threw	thrown	*atirar, lançar*
wake up	woke up	woken up	*acordar, despertar*
wear	wore	worn	*vestir, usar*
write	wrote	written	*escrever*

Language reference

Chapter 1 — "Will" x "going to" (review)

O *future simple* é formado pelo verbo auxiliar *will* + a forma infinitiva sem a partícula *to* (forma básica) do verbo principal. A forma contraída é: *'ll* + verbo principal.

A forma interrogativa segue o padrão de deslocar o verbo auxiliar para antes do sujeito. Isso vale tanto para *yes/no questions* (*will* + sujeito + verbo principal + complemento) quanto para perguntas com *wh- words* (*what*, *where*, *why* etc.):

Will you **come** to my party?

When **will** they **hand in** their papers?

Na forma negativa, pode-se utilizar *will not* ou a contração *won't*:

He **will not/won't** have time to do all his tasks.

O *future simple* é utilizado para expressar previsões com base em opinião ou experiência pessoal. Também pode ser usado para:

- fazer uma promessa:

  I promise I**'ll do** my best.

- expressar um fato:

  She **will finish** high school next year.

- fazer uma solicitação:

  Will you **help** me, please?

- oferecer-se para fazer algo:

  I**'ll help** you write your résumé.

- expressar uma decisão tomada no momento:

  Someone's knocking at the door! I**'ll open** it.

- expressar um sonho:

  I**'ll be** a billionaire one day.

O futuro com *going to*, na forma afirmativa, é formado pelo verbo *to be* no *present simple* + *going to* + verbo principal no infinitivo sem a partícula *to*.

A forma negativa é formada pelo verbo *to be* no *simple present* + *not* + *going to* + verbo principal no infinitivo sem a partícula *to*.

A forma interrogativa com *going to* segue, também, o padrão de deslocar o verbo auxiliar para antes do sujeito, procedimento que vale tanto para *yes/no questions* (verbo *to be* no *present simple* + sujeito + *going to* + verbo principal + complemento) quanto para perguntas com *wh- words* (*what*, *where*, *why* etc.):

Is she **going to talk** to the principal in the afternoon?

Where **are** you **going to live** when you go to college?

O futuro com *going to* é usado para:

- expressar um propósito bem definido:

  I**'m going to help** you do well in your job interview.

- expressar uma previsão com base em evidências:
  You are very sociable. You're going to enjoy working with different people.
- perguntar sobre planos futuros:
  What are you going to do this weekend?
- expressar planos ou intenções:
  Aren't you going to study for the test tonight?

Chapter 2 — Conditional sentences – types zero and 1

As orações condicionais são empregadas quando se deseja estabelecer uma relação entre uma condição e um resultado, podendo se referir a situações reais, hipotéticas ou não realizáveis.

Observe no quadro a relação entre a condição e o que resulta dessa condição no presente:

Condition: *If* + present tense	Result: in the present
If you **heat** metal,	it **expands**.

Observe agora a relação entre a condição e o resultado que se espera no futuro:

Condition: *If* + present tense	Result: in the future
If it **rains**,	we **will stay home** tomorrow.

Chapter 3 — Expressing obligation and recommendation ("have to", "must", "should")

Para falar sobre obrigações e deveres, utiliza-se *have to* ou *must*.

*She **has to** finish everything by 2 o'clock.*

*We **must** make a decision today.*

Quando *have to* e *must* são usados na forma negativa, expressam sentidos diferentes. *Don't have to* expressa a não necessidade de algo, ao passo que *mustn't* expressa uma proibição.

*You **don't have to** bring your Math book to school tomorrow.*

*You **mustn't** drive faster than 50 km/h in this area.*

Utiliza-se *should* para dar conselhos e sugestões ou para fazer recomendações.

*I think you **should** eat less sugar.*

Affirmative	Negative	Interrogative
I **have to** go now.	I **don't have to** go now.	**Do** I **have to** go now?
He **must sleep** now.	He **mustn't sleep** now.	**Must** he **sleep** now?
We **should wait** here.	We **shouldn't wait** here.	**Should** we **wait** here?

Chapter 4 — Modals of probability ("may", "might", "will")

Os verbos modais *may* e *might* são usados para falar de fatos possíveis ou prováveis de acontecer.

May é usado para mencionar um evento ou uma ação com uma possibilidade grande de acontecer, se estiver na forma afirmativa, ou de não acontecer, se estiver na forma negativa.

Might expressa uma probabilidade mais remota, não tão certa de ocorrer.

*The traffic is terrible today. We **may** be late for our appointment.*

*She **might** go to the beach if she gets some days off next month.*

May e *might* possuem em comum a característica de manter a mesma forma para todos os sujeitos, não sofrendo alterações na 3ª pessoa do singular (*he*, *she*, *it*). Após esses verbos modais, o verbo principal estará sempre no infinitivo sem a partícula *to*.

Usa-se *will* para falar sobre previsões com base em opiniões e experiências prévias. Assim como os modais *may* e *might*, *will* não apresenta variação na sua forma, sendo a mesma para todas as pessoas, e, na forma afirmativa, é seguido pelo verbo no infinitivo sem a partícula *to*.

Diferentemente de *may* e *might*, que expressam uma probabilidade maior ou menor, as previsões feitas com *will* expressam certeza com base em opiniões e experiências prévias.

*I'm sure you'**ll do** just fine in your presentation.*

Chapter 5 — Present perfect with "for" and "since"

O *present perfect* é empregado para expressar:

- ações que aconteceram no passado, em um tempo não definido:
  *Mary **has arrived**.*

- ações iniciadas no passado que se estendem até o presente:
  *Inflation **has gone up** in recent years.*

- ações que ocorreram muitas vezes no passado:
  *I **have read** that book many times.*

O *present perfect* é formado pelo auxiliar *have* seguido do particípio passado do verbo principal. É importante lembrar que, na 3ª pessoa do singular, o auxiliar é flexionado (*has*).

Affirmative	Negative	Interrogative
They **have called** you.	They **haven't called** you.	**Have** they **called** you?
She **has left** early.	She **hasn't left** early.	**Has** she **left** early?

Para indicar desde quando uma ação vem ocorrendo, usa-se o advérbio de tempo *since*.

*We have lived here **since** 2015.*

Para indicar há quanto tempo uma ação vem ocorrendo, usa-se o advérbio de tempo *for*.

*They have lived in London **for** 5 years.*

Chapter 6 — Present perfect with "ever", "already", "yet" and "never"

O *present perfect* também pode ser usado com as expressões de tempo *ever*, *already*, *yet* and *never*.

Questions	Affirmative answers	Negative answers
Has he **ever** been to Paris?	Yes, he has **already** been to Paris.	No, he has **never** been to Paris. No, he hasn't been to Paris **yet**.
Have they **already** met Bill?	Yes, they have **already** met him.	No, they haven't met him **yet**.

Chapter 7 — Present simple x past simple x present perfect

Observe as diferenças de uso entre *present simple*, *past simple* e *present perfect*:

Present simple	Past simple	Present perfect
Utilizado para falar sobre rotinas e atividades diárias.	Utilizado para falar sobre ações que começaram e terminaram em um momento específico no passado.	Utilizado para se referir a ações no passado com consequência no presente. Utilizado para expressar ações que começaram no passado e continuam no presente. Utilizado para falar sobre fatos ou eventos que começaram em um momento no passado (o momento específico não é importante ou é desconhecido).

Chapter 8 — Conditional sentences – type 2

As orações condicionais do tipo 2 são empregadas quando se deseja estabelecer uma relação entre uma condição hipotética e um possível resultado, também hipotético:

Condition: *If* + past simple	Result: *would* + verb in the basic form
If you **asked** me,	I **would help** you.

As orações condicionais do tipo 2 também podem ser feitas com outras conjunções além de *if*.

Result: *would* + verb in the basic form	Condition: *unless/even if* + past simple verb
We **would not be** able to see the show	**unless** we had the tickets in our hand.
They **would go** to the beach	**even if** it rained.

Interdisciplinary project
The spread of English across the world

Presentation

Vamos investigar a expansão da língua inglesa pelo mundo como resultado da colonização britânica e os papéis que o idioma desempenha em diversas áreas.

Procedures

Part I (History, English and Arts)

Objective: discuss the spread of the English language across the world as a result of British colonization.

Resources: atlas, History books, internet (research papers, review articles, documentaries etc.).

Instructions

a. Formem quatro grupos. Coletem informações sobre como o processo de colonização britânica se desenvolveu ao redor do mundo. Cada grupo deve se concentrar em um continente: América, África, Ásia e Oceania.

b. Revisem todas as informações que vocês já coletaram sobre esse assunto nos projetos realizados nos anos anteriores.

c. Descubram quando, por que e como os colonizadores britânicos chegaram à parte do mundo que vocês estão pesquisando. Organizem as informações cronologicamente.

d. Reúnam a maior quantidade possível de informações sobre as características do lugar na época da conquista britânica: ele já tinha sido colonizado por outros povos? Seus habitantes tentaram resistir de alguma forma? Que idiomas eram falados nesse território? Que culturas já existiam lá? Seus habitantes já haviam colonizado outros lugares?

Analysis

1. É possível concluir que a colonização dos lugares pesquisados trouxe benefícios aos povos conquistados? 2. Ela causou algum dano às culturas locais?? Por exemplo, contribuiu para a extinção de línguas locais ou impôs alguma restrição linguística?

Reflections

1. Por que o processo de colonização variava de um lugar para outro? 2. Por que esses países foram colonizados pelos britânicos e não por outros povos?

Part II (History and English)

Objective: discuss intercultural communication through English.

Resources: History books, internet (research papers, review articles, documentaries etc.).

Instructions

a. Reúnam-se com o mesmo grupo da atividade anterior. Coletem informações sobre os fatores históricos que ajudaram a moldar o conceito de globalização que conhecemos hoje.

b. Pensem no papel da língua inglesa no processo de globalização. Com a ajuda do/a professor/a de Língua Inglesa, respondam a estas perguntas com a maior quantidade possível de informações:

Analysis

1. Qual é o número de pessoas no mundo que têm o inglês como língua nativa? E como segunda língua ou língua adicional? 2. O que isso indica em relação à importância da consciência cultural para a eficácia da comunicação em um mundo globalizado?

1. Quem mais usa o inglês, além dos falantes nativos? 2. Como as variedades do inglês impactam a comunicação entre pessoas de diferentes países? 3. Qual é o papel da cultura na interação entre pessoas que usam a língua inglesa?

Reflections

1. O que é mais importante: a proficiência na língua inglesa ou a competência comunicativa intercultural? 2. O aprendizado da língua inglesa melhora o conhecimento de mundo e de suas diversas culturas? Como? 3. É possível assumir uma identidade fixa em um mundo multicultural?

Part III (English and History)

Objective: analyze the importance of the English language for the development of the sciences, economy and politics.

Resources: newspapers, magazines, books, internet.

Instructions

a Reúnam-se com o mesmo grupo das atividades anteriores e analisem a importância da língua inglesa no desenvolvimento das ciências e da economia em uma perspectiva global.

b Formulem uma hipótese com base no que descobriram nas *Parts* I e II. Proponham uma explicação para o fato de o inglês ter se tornado globalmente importante no desenvolvimento das ciências e da economia.

c Comecem a pesquisa considerando os seguintes tópicos:

I número de falantes nativos e de pessoas que falam inglês como segunda língua ou língua adicional no mundo;

II porcentagem de artigos científicos publicados em inglês no mundo;

III países em que estão localizadas as universidades mais influentes do mundo;

IV universidades que possuem o maior número de estudantes estrangeiros;

V países cujas decisões nas áreas de ciências e economia exercem maior influência sobre outras nações.

Analysis

1. Sua hipótese inicial se confirmou? 2. Dos países que apareceram em sua pesquisa, quais têm o inglês como língua nativa ou oficial? 3. Vocês acham que o grande número de estudantes que procuram programas universitários em inglês tem relação com a grande quantidade de artigos publicados nesse idioma?

Reflections

1. Quais podem ser os aspectos negativos do uso de um único idioma na divulgação de conhecimentos e como essa desvantagem poderia ser solucionada? 2. Considerando que, ao longo da história, outras línguas desempenharam o papel ocupado hoje pelo inglês, vocês acham que o *status* desse idioma como língua universal das ciências pode mudar um dia?

Sharing knowledge

Compartilhem os resultados do seu projeto com a comunidade escolar. Vocês podem planejar uma apresentação para a vizinhança e, assim, ampliar esse público.

Instructions

a Peçam aos/às professores/professoras que participaram do projeto que revisem e ajustem as informações coletadas pelo grupo. Essa validação será particularmente importante para garantir a precisão do material.

b Preparem a versão final da apresentação. Decidam como organizar e exibir os resultados do projeto.

Presentation

Com a supervisão dos/as professores/professoras, apresentem seus resultados à comunidade escolar.

Assessment

Avaliem a experiência que vocês tiveram nessa investigação científica, considerando, entre outros aspectos: colaboração, respeito, criatividade, imaginação, resolução de problemas, habilidades e iniciativa.

Transcripts

Chapter 1

Track 3 – Page 17

The world of work is changing. It's no longer a place where we go or where we come from. Work is wherever we need it to be. Tablet and smartphone adoption is growing by 50% every year. Mobile technology means change that goes way beyond working at the coffee shop or the kitchen table. This is a revolution enabling anyone to now work flexibly and effectively, anytime, anywhere. [...] 357% more businesses are offering mobile working options, and 70% of employees prefer to work remotely. Employees longing to be more productive, but also longing for a smaller commute and a greater work-life balance are becoming free-range. We're no longer governed by the nine-to-five, leaving the house at 6 to be in a claustrophobic cube tethered to a fixed line, but instead, with the flexibility to break free, we're choosing where, when and how we work. Work can now be done anywhere: from home, from the road, from airports, motorway services, railway stations, retail outlets, from hubs closer to that first meeting at the start of the day and closer to home at the end of it. Mobile workers are more connected, more motivated, more productive and get more quality time with family and friends with over half of working parents saying family relationships improve whilst working flexibly.

Extract from the audio available at <https://www.youtube.com/watch?v=ejb63HgT-s4>. Accessed on May 22, 2019.

Chapter 2

Track 4 (Track 5: Part 2; Track 6: Part 3) – Page 29

Part 1

May-Li: Computers are everywhere! They are in people's pockets, they are in people's cars, people have them on their wrists, they might be in your backpack right now. But what makes a computer a computer?

Nat: What does make a computer a computer, anyway?

May-Li: And how does it even work?

Part 2

Nat: [...] As humans, we've always built tools to help us solve problems. Tools like a wheelbarrow, a hammer or a printing press or a tractor trailer. All of these inventions helped us with manual work. Over time, people began to wonder if a machine could be designed and built to help us with the thinking work we do, like, solving equations or tracking the stars in the sky. Rather than moving or manipulating physical things like dirt and stone, these machines would need to be designed to manipulate information.

May-Li: As the pioneers of computer science explored how to design a thinking machine, they realized that it had to perform four different tasks. It would need to take input, store information, process it and then output the results. Now this might sound simple, but these four things are common to all computers. That's what makes a computer a computer.

Part 3

Nat: The earliest computers were made out of wood and metal with mechanical levers and gears. By the 20th century, though, computers started using electrical components. These early computers were really large and really slow. A computer the size of a room might take hours just to do a basic math problem. [...]

May-Li: Computers started out as basic calculators, which was already really awesome at the time, and they were only manipulating numbers back then. But now we can use them to talk to each other, we can use them to play games, control robots and do any crazy thing that you can probably imagine.

Nat: Modern computers look nothing like those clunky old machines, but they still do the same four things.

Extracts from the audio available at <https://www.youtube.com/watch?v=mCq8-xTH7jA>. Accessed on May 22, 2019.

Chapter 3

Track 7 – Page 42

Hello, everybody. [...] Today we are talking about a form of government that is really important here in the United States. It is a democracy. Now, democracy started in Athens, Greece, but like most city-states, it did not start as a democracy. It actually started as a monarchy, where you've got one person in charge. After a while, in Athens people got tired of having one person in charge and the rich people in Athens took over, took control from the monarchy and developed a government where there were only a few people in charge, and these were the rich landowners in Athens. We call that type of government an oligarchy – and if you're being more specific, a government where you have the rich people in charge, that would be an aristocracy. But we'll stick with oligarchy from now on. Now, like most times, you have power in a small number of people, those people become very powerful and other people don't like that. [...] The laws in Athens became very strict. [...] Eventually, some very powerful individuals were able to gather an army together and overthrow the oligarchy. The first guy's name to do this was Pisistratus. [...] He did take over and he was known as a tyrant – the type of government is a tyranny. So, it's a very different meaning today. In ancient Greece, a tyrant was somebody who took control with power. Today, we usually think of tyrants as being people who rule unfairly. Tyrants came and tyrants went, different tyrants rose up and took control and then lost control. Eventually, the people in Athens had had enough and they created a style of government that would influence the United States today. We call that democracy. Democracy comes from two Greek terms that basically mean the power of the people. Democracy is where people get to vote on the laws that govern them.

Extract from the audio available at <https://www.youtube.com/watch?v=4JWGBMAgjqs>. Accessed on May 22, 2019.

Track 8 – Page 43

[...] So, let's take a look at the differences between Athens and the United States today. They both have democracies, but those democracies are very different. First of all, in Athens, the democracy was what is known as a direct democracy, and what that means is that all citizens got together and debated issues and laws. And then voted on those issues and laws. All citizens, all laws. In the United States it is a little bit different. Can you imagine if we voted on every single law? Plus, we are a lot bigger than Athens, Greece. So, in the United States we have what is called the representative democracy. What that means is we vote for other people who, then, go to Washington, D.C. to vote on laws for us. That means every time there's a law, I don't have to go to Washington, D.C. myself and vote for it. My senators, my representatives do that for me. In Athens, Greece, there was no separation of power. Citizens would create laws, they would enforce the laws, they would be judges. In the United States is a little bit different. We've got what are called Checks and Balances. [...] We've got three branches of government: we've got the legislative branch of government – it's congress, that's the senate, the house of representatives – they're the ones that make the laws. We've got the executive branch: that's the president and one of the president's big roles is to enforce those laws. And then we've got the judicial branch. The judicial branches are all the courts in the United States. Their job is to interpret the laws and judge the laws. Decide whether laws are fair, whether laws are legal, and then decide whether people are innocent or guilty. Finally, in Athens, Greece, only free males from Athens could vote. In the United States we know it's a lot different than that: men can vote, women can vote, people who come into the country and get citizenship can vote – much different than Athens, Greece. We also know that in the United States that was not always the way it worked. So, we've moved along to allow more people to vote. So, while Athens' democracy is much different than in the United States, they were the first step towards the type of government we've got today in the United States.

Extract from the audio available at <https://www.youtube.com/watch?v=4JWGBMAgjqs>. Accessed on May 22, 2019.

Track 9 – Page 55

Excerpt 1

Can a bunch of primary school kids really change the world? Well, we're gonna try.

Hi, I'm Coulter, and my class and I have split into teams and we're gonna spend the first five minutes of school every day this week changing the world.

At our house, we have heaps of old mobiles lying around – and across Australia, they reckon there are about 10 million – and the parts can all be recycled. So we've asked every kid in school to bring in their old mobiles and we have five minutes to pick them up.

Mobiles have these really poisonous chemicals in them and when we chuck them out with the garbage, the chemicals go into the water and soil and end up in our food.

Excerpt 2

Hi, I'm Dana [...].

This morning my group has two challenges. First, we have to weed our garden and plant new veggies. Then we have to feed our whole class. And we only have three minutes left. Tuesday is our Munch 'n Crunch day, where [sic] local growers donate fruit and veg for us to eat, but today we are adding stuff from our own garden.

Excerpt 3

Hey, I'm Brigitte and today me and my group are on a mission to turn off all the electrical stuff in the school that's not being used, 'cause it's not like you can deny global warming anymore, and wasting power is one of the big planet warmers.

Excerpt 4

Hi, I'm Gabby. Most kids in my class say they want new toys, games and books and things like that, but they also think they've got a whole bunch of stuff they don't want anymore. So rather than chuck things into landfill and buy new stuff, our group has organized everybody to bring in something and we're having a 5-minute free garage sale. An Aussie family of four generates nearly 7 tons of waste every year, which is a third more than we did 10 years ago.

Extracts from the audio available at <https://www.youtube.com/watch?v=oROsbaxWH0M>. Accessed on May 27, 2019.

Track 10 (Track 11: Part 1; Track 12: Part 2) – Pages 68-69

Part 1

Arthur Mutambara: Climate change, [...] globalization, nuclear weapons, terrorism, poverty... All these global challenges are interconnected. You can't solve the issues around climate change without addressing global poverty. You can't solve the issues around terrorism without addressing the issue of human rights. It is imperative for all global players to understand that we must be seeking a global victory. We must be seeking global success. Yes, maybe you can't concentrate on all the challenges. But as you address climate change as a problem, realize that climate change is linked to poverty. It's linked to human rights. It's linked to nuclear weapons as a challenge. And so, we need more holistic models; more encompassing, unified approaches in terms of addressing global challenges. So that's my major concern; because when I listen to my friends in America and my friends in Europe, they seem to have this atomic approach to challenges where they are so concerned about global warming and climate change. And they do not, in the same breath, discuss about a starving peasant in Somalia.

A starving peasant in Somalia cannot have a green agenda; cannot think about global warming. They will eat grass. They will cause deforestation because they have to survive. So, if you are serious about addressing climate change, you must, at the same time, address issues around poverty. So, in summary, all global challenges are interconnected. You can't solve one challenge without addressing the other. [...]

Part 2

You can't have success in Japan when there's failure in Somalia and Zimbabwe. You can't have success in America when there's chaos in Iraq and Cuba. We must pursue global success. We must pursue global victory. Climate change affects all countries, so you can't fix climate change in America without fixing climate change in Sudan.

Extracts from the audio available at <https://www.youtube.com/watch?v=9Tea9ckMIZc>. Accessed on May 22, 2019.

Track 13 – Page 81

For most of history, the overwhelming majority of the Earth's inhabitants have owned more or less nothing. The clothes they stood up in, some bowls, a pot and a pan, perhaps a broom and, if things were going really well, a few farming implements. Nations and peoples remained consistently poor. Global GDP did not grow at all from year to year. The world was an aggregate as hard up in 1800 as it had been at the beginning of time. However, starting in the early 18th century, in the countries of Northwestern Europe, a remarkable phenomenon occurred. Economies began to expand and wages to rise. Families, who'd never before had any money beyond what they needed just to survive, found they could go shopping for small luxuries: a comb or a mirror, a spare set of underwear, a pillow, some thicker boots or a towel. Their expenditure created a virtuous economic cycle. The more they spent, the more businesses grew, the more wages rose. By the middle of the 18th century, observers recognized that they were living through a period of epochal change that historians have since described as the world's first consumer revolution.

Extract from the audio available at <https://www.youtube.com/watch?v=Y-Unq3R--M0>. Accessed on May 27, 2019.

Chapter 7

Track 14 – Page 95

Interviewer: So, you're blind, you must not be racist, right?

Speaker 1: I am racist. [...] I am racist because I think every white person is racist. I participate in institutions, like I benefit from capitalism which was built on slavery and racism. [...] Like, seeing someone's skin color, I think, is not the only way that we differentiate people's, like, culture or race. [...]

Speaker 2: I... No. [...] You know, we don't necessarily go around asking: "are you black?", "are you white?", you know? You are who you are as far as I'm concerned. [...] I've had experiences where I've known, you know, a person for probably a year, year and half or so, and they never knew I was black. Ironically this was another black person. They were like: "you're black?" and I was: "yeah, yeah, I'm black", so... [...]

Speaker 3: No. [...] Blindness does sometimes take those racial cues out of society, because if I can't tell by someone's voice or accent or whatever, like, I have no idea. [...]

Speaker 4: No. [...] Because I can't see. [...]

Speaker 5: I would like to think that I'm not. However, there are those stereotypes that have been instilled in everyone. [...] I can pick a dialect and sometimes try to associate them with what race they might be. I wish I could just completely just ignore it. But I can't help it. If I'm walking down the street and I hear a couple of people and they are, like, aggressively talking to each other and it's slang and vulgar speech and it's not eloquent, I naturally sometimes think "Oh, those people might be black because of their accent". I shouldn't think like that, but there are natural stereotypes out there in the world.

Extracts from the audio available at <https://www.youtube.com/watch?v=uqoFsqOJYCg>. Accessed on May 22, 2019.

Track 15 — Page 106

Bill Sternberg: Events at the University of Missouri in the past week have raised a number of interesting issues, ranging from racism on campus to the power of the college football teams, whether the administrators deserve to be pushed out or run out by a mob, to the limits of free speech on campus, in Missouri and elsewhere. Saundra, where do you think we should go with all of this?

Extract from the audio available at <https://www.youtube.com/watch?v=Z_IZ3kAfz4I>. Accessed on May 22, 2019.

Track 16 — Page 107

Saundra Torry: One conclusion I've come to of many is that universities, I think, should now have a required class in their freshman year in the First Amendment and free speech. I mean, you have a right to say what you want, but again it's been said in editorials, you don't necessarily have a right if somebody's fired from a radio station or network for saying things that people find offensive. [...]

Eileen Rivers: If Mizzou was just about people yelling the n-word, then I would agree with you. [...] Mizzou was also about systemic racism built within the college structure. [...] This was also about students on video, this is a video that's gone viral, confronting the president and saying, of the university, and saying: "Do you know what systemic racism is?" And his response was: "Yes, it's when you people feel like you're not getting what you want". [...] That's a president that has no idea how to deal with race; that's a president that has no idea how to address an entire student body and, to me, that says that that is racism from the top down that affects how students are educated and how they are treated.

Thuan Elston: I mean, I agree with you that, that Tim Wolf, Wolf has no right to be a president of a university system if he can't, if he doesn't recognize that there is systemic racism and he doesn't know how to handle the situation with students in trying to show everybody that he's there to protect everybody, to look out for all students. But that's separate from the First Amendment issue on campus grounds. [...]

David Mastio: Right, there's a few facts that we have to keep in mind and that is that this is a campus that is so racist, so full of hate, that a black gay man was elected student body president, you know, landslide.

Eileen: That's the equivalent of saying "since Obama is president, he's black, racism is over". Come on!

David: No one said racism is over. It's about keeping things in perspective.

Extracts from the audio available at <https://www.youtube.com/watch?v=Z_IZ3kAfz4I>. Accessed on May 22, 2019.

Glossary

CHAPTER 1

A
accountant: contador/a
acknowledge: identificar, reconhecer
advisor: consultor/a
aim: objetivo
application: inscrição
arrangement: disposição, organização
Associate's (degree): graduação em curso superior de curta duração, semelhante ao curso tecnólogo

B
Bachelor's (degree): bacharelado
brickmason/blockmason: pedreiro/a
bureau: departamento, escritório

C
carry out: conduzir, realizar
cover letter: carta de apresentação

D
Doctoral (degree): doutorado

E
employee: funcionário/a
employment: emprego
environment: meio ambiente

F
fill out: preencher
footnote: nota de rodapé
freight: frete

G
gender: gênero, sexo

H
healthcare: cuidados com a saúde

I
increase: aumento
insurance: seguro

K
key: legenda (para identificar elementos de um gráfico)

M
management: administração, gerenciamento, gestão
Master's (degree): mestrado

N
nurse: enfermeiro/a

O
occupation: profissão

R
rate: taxa
retrieve: recuperar

S
sales: vendas
scatter plot: diagrama de dispersão
schedule: horário
slice: fatia
stand out: destacar-se
submission email: *e-mail* de apresentação
surgeon: cirurgião/cirurgiã

T
tailor: fazer sob medida
thousand: mil, milhar
trend: tendência

W
warehousing: armazenamento
wholesale: venda de atacado

CHAPTER 2

A
awesome: incrível

B
backlash: reação negativa
brain: cérebro

C
clause: oração (gramática)
closer: mais próximo/a

D
dirt: terra

E
even if: mesmo se

F
farm: fazenda

H
headmaster: diretor (de escola)
headmistress: diretora (de escola)

I
infotainment: infoentretenimento
input: inserir; entrada de dados

L
limb: membro (do corpo)

M
mind: importar-se

O
otherwise: de outra forma, do contrário

P
prosthetic: protético/a
pupil: estudante
purposefully: intencionalmente

R
rooftop: cobertura (de edifício), telhado

S
self-check-in kiosk: painel de autoatendimento para fazer *check-in*
skip: pular
stone: pedra
summarize: resumir

T
take a break: fazer uma pausa
task: tarefa
tip: dica
tooth: dente

U
unless: a não ser que

W
waste: desperdício
wheelbarrow: carrinho de mão

CHAPTER 3

B
back talk: resposta insolente
blame: culpar

C
charity: beneficente; caridade
citizenship: cidadania

D
disadvantaged: desfavorecido/a
drainage: drenagem

E
eco-friendly: ecologicamente correto
enforce: impor

F
fellow citizen: concidadão

I
instill: instilar

K
king: rei

L
landowner: proprietário/a de terras
lift: levantar
litter: jogar lixo em lugar inapropriado, sujar
look after: cuidar

O
obey: obedecer
overthrow: destituir

P
principle: causa primária, princípio
priority seat: assento preferencial

Q
queen: rainha

R
revere: admirar, venerar

S
spoiled: mimado/a
stand up for: defender

T
take over: assumir o controle
tax: imposto
thought: pensamento
thumb: polegar

Y
yell: gritar

CHAPTER 4

B
blockage: obstrução

C
chuck out (informal): jogar fora
cleanup: mutirão de limpeza

D
dispose: descartar

E
end up: acabar, ir parar
engine: motor
entity: entidade

F
faucet: torneira
float: flutuar
foresight: previsão
fuel: combustível

G
global warming: aquecimento global
grammarian: gramático/a
greenhouse: estufa
grower: agricultor/a

K
kill: matar

L
landfill: aterro
last: durar
light bulb: lâmpada
loss: perda

N
neat: organizado/a

P
poisonous: tóxico/a, venenoso/a

R
recover: recuperar
recycling bin: lixeira de reciclagem
renewable: renovável
round trip: ida e volta

S
scarcity: escassez
soil: solo
stopwatch: cronômetro
store: armazenar, guardar
stream: riacho
sum: soma

T
throw away: jogar fora
trash: lixo

U
unsold: não vendido/a
up to date: atualizado/a

W
weed: remover ervas daninhas
wisely: sabiamente

CHAPTER 5

A
argue: argumentar
assess: avaliar

D
deforestation: desmatamento
deny: negar

E
engage: envolver-se com

F
failure: fracasso
fix: consertar
for: a favor; por; para
former: antigo/a; anterior

H
however: no entanto

K
keep track: acompanhar, registrar
knowledge: conhecimento

L
lead: levar
long run: longo prazo

M
medium: meio, modo

O
outperform: sair-se melhor, superar

P
peer: igual, par
poor: pobre
poverty: pobreza
pretend: fingir
pursue: buscar, perseguir

Q
quote: citação; citar

S
side: lado
starvation: fome, inanição
supporter: torcedor/a

T
take turns: revezar-se
therefore: portanto
towards: em relação a
trade: comércio

W
wealth: riqueza
weapon: arma
western: ocidental

CHAPTER 6

A
advertisement (ad): anúncio publicitário
aircraft: aeronave
automated teller machine (ATM): caixa eletrônico

B
billboard: *outdoor* (anglicismo)
broom: vassoura

C
cash: dinheiro em espécie
celebrity branding: endosso por celebridade
charge: cobrança
coin: moeda
comb: pente
consumer: consumidor/a
currency: moeda corrente

D
desired: desejado/a
direct mail: mala direta

F
farming implement: ferramenta de agricultura
flight attendant: comissário/a de bordo

G
gift card: vale-presente
grab: atrair, prender
groceries: gêneros alimentícios, mantimentos

H
hardly ever: raramente
hum: cantar com os lábios fechados, cantarolar

I
inextricable: indissociável, inextricável
installment: parcela, prestação
interest: juros

L
lend: emprestar

M
make-believe: de faz de conta
manufacturer: fabricante
mend: consertar, reparar

P
pan: panela
pattern: padrão
pillow: travesseiro
pot: vaso
purchase: compra

R
remarkable: extraordinário

S
sandwich board sign: cartaz-sanduíche
sewing machine: máquina de costura
shade: tom
shelter: abrigo
shopping cart: carrinho de compras
skip the ad: pular o anúncio
sooner: antes
split: dividir
surrogate: substituto/a

T
target: alvo
towel: toalha
truthfulness: veracidade
typist: digitador/a

W
wage: salário
withdraw: sacar (dinheiro)

CHAPTER 7

A
accent: sotaque
appeal: apelo

B
beat: espancar
blind: cego/a
bullet: bala, projétil

C
charge: acusação
choke: enforcar
clash: conflito
courtroom: tribunal
coverage: cobertura
cupboard: armário

D
demonstrator: manifestante
disgraceful: vergonhoso

E
emergency ward: pronto-socorro

G
gripping: arrebatador/a, cativante

H
headquarters: matriz, sede
hideout: esconderijo
hire: contratar
hole: buraco
homelessness: desabrigo

I
indeed: de fato

J
jam: geleia
judge: julgar

L
law enforcement: polícia
loiter: ficar em um local sem motivo
lone: solitário/a, sozinho/a

M
marcher: manifestante
matter: importar; questão

P
polite: educado/a
powerful: poderoso/a
prod: estimular

R
remind: lembrar
resemble: assemelhar-se, parecer

S
seek: procurar
sewage: esgoto
shot: baleado/a
shut down: fechar
stirring: estimulante
storm into: invadir
sympathy: aprovação, empatia, solidariedade

T
touchstone: pedra de toque, ponto de referência

CHAPTER 8

A
abiding: duradouro/a, permanente
abridge: abreviar
allow: permitir
apologize: desculpar-se
approval: aprovação
assemble: reunir-se
assembly: assembleia

B
badly: extremamente
board: conselho, diretoria
built within: enraizado/a

C
censorship: censura
character: caractere
claim: afirmar
close in: fechar o cerco
clumsy: desajeitado/a
complain: reclamar
customer: cliente

D
deep: profundo/a

E
exchange: intercâmbio, troca

F
first amendment: primeira emenda
freedom of speech: liberdade de expressão

G
grievance: injustiça, queixa

I
inadvertently: inadvertidamente

O
on board with: de acordo com

P
policy: política

R
rage: agir com raiva ou fúria
redress: reforma, retificação
renowned: conhecido/a
resignation: exoneração

S
settle: chegar a um acordo, resolver
shorten: encurtar
speak one's mind: dizer o que pensa
suffragette: sufragista
supposedly: supostamente

T
take a stand: tomar uma posição
turning point: momento decisivo

U
unfortunately: infelizmente

W
wisdom: sabedoria

Learning more

Chapter 1

What Color Is Your Parachute? – for Teens

Written by Carol Christen, Jean M. Blomquist and Richard N. Bolles. United States: Ten Speed Press, 2015.

There comes a time in life when we are surrounded by difficult questions and bombarded with hard decisions to make. One of them is about our career choices for the future, and this book can help you decide. *What Color Is Your Parachute? – for Teens* is an age-appropriate version of the book *What Color Is Your Parachute?*, published in 1970. The book promises to inform teens about college, majors, careers and the work market, always through an approach that will appeal to the young audience.

Chapter 2

Computer History Museum

Computers are an essential part of our daily lives, and sometimes it can be hard to imagine how things were done before their invention. But have you ever thought about how long it took for our personal computers to become what they are today? In the Computer History Museum official website you can follow a timeline through the computer history, from the first attempts to preserve data to the modern-day lightweight computers.

Chapter 3

Suffragette

Produced by Alison Owen. United Kingdom, France: Ruby Films, Pathé, Film4, 2015.

Nowadays, in most countries, it is common to see men and women voting to choose the representatives of their country. However, for many centuries, women could not take part in such an important decision process. In this movie, Maud Watts, a working mother from 1912 London, decides to fight for a change in society, showing the inequality between genders in many aspects of her daily life.

Chapter 4

Plastic Planet

Produced by Thomas Bogner. Austria, Germany: Neue Sentimental Film, 2009.

Look around you and try to tell what material is present in almost every object you can see. The answer will probably be plastic. This documentary shows how prevalent plastic is in the lives of people in 25 countries and how this can be harmful to the health of human beings and to nature.

Chapter 5

1493: From Columbus's Voyage to Globalization – For Young People

Written by Charles C. Mann; adapted by Rebecca Stefoff. New York: Triangle Square, 2016.

If you think globalization is a recent invention, you might be wrong. Believe it or not, the process to what we know today as globalization actually started over 500 years ago, when people decided to travel around the world in search of new and undiscovered places, creating relationships that had never existed before. This book depicts, in an easily understandable way, how globalization has been changing cultures and peoples since then.

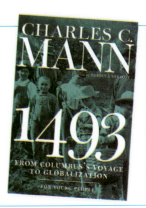

Chapter 6

The Story of Stuff Project – Podcast

The Story of Stuff Project is based on the famous video *The Story of Stuff*, which summarizes, with an easy language, how consumerism works. This podcast, available on the project's official website, discusses related topics, such as sustainable consumption, animal protection, recycling and climate change. And if after listening to the podcast you feel an intense desire to take action, the website also offers you several projects in which you can take part.

Chapter 7

Long Walk to Freedom – The Autobiography of Nelson Mandela

Written by Nelson Mandela. Boston: Back Bay Books, 1994.

This autobiography written by the first black president of South Africa, Nelson Mandela, retells the story of his life, since childhood, through law school and, finally, until his fight against apartheid. Because of this fight, Mandela unjustly spent 28 years of his life in prison, but the battle he had taken part in was carried on by many other South Africans and, when he was finally released from prison, in 1990, apartheid was in its final moments. In 1994, he was elected president of South Africa.

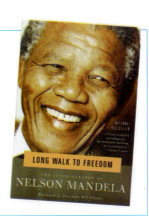

Chapter 8

Forbidden Voices – How to Start a Revolution with a Laptop

Produced by Philip Delaquis. Switzerland: Das Kollektiv für audiovisuelle Werke GmbH, 2012.

Do you have a blog? What do you think people use blogs for? For most people, blogs are used to discuss opinions on topics such as movies, books etc., but for Yoani, Zeng and Farnaz, a blog can be an instrument to reveal what their countries try to censor. This documentary shows how these three women use their blogs to fight repression in Cuba, China and Iran, facing surveillance, arrests and even violence.

143

Track list

Track	Chapter	Activity	Page
1	Introduction	-	-
2	1	2	17
3	1	3	17
4	2	2	29
5	2	3	29
6	2	4	29
7	3	2, 3	42
8	3	4, 5	43
9	4	2, 3	55
10	5	2	68
11	5	3	69
12	5	4	69
13	6	3, 4	81
14	7	3, 4	95
15	8	2	106
16	8	3, 4	107

References

BODDEN, Valerie. *Identify and Evaluate Advertising*. Minneapolis: Lerner Publications, 2015.

CHAUDHARY, Anjali Y. *The Impact of Television Advertising on Children*. Solapur: Laxmi Book Publication, 2016.

FAIR, Bryan K. *Notes of a Racial Caste Baby:* **Color Blindness and the End of Affirmative Action**. New York; London: New York University Press, 1997.

FRANK, Anne. *The Diary of a Young Girl*. New York: Doubleday, 1995.

GOLD, Harry J. *The Digital Advertising Guide*. Allston: Overdrive Marketing Communications, 2015.

HAMILTON, Sara M. *Globalization*. Edina: ABDO Publishing, 2009.

KEARL, Holly. *Stop Street Harassment:* **Making Public Places Safe and Welcoming for Women**. Santa Barbara: ABC-CLIO, 2010.

LOCKARD, Craig A. *Societies, Networks, and Transitions:* **A Global History**. 2 ed. Stamford: Wadsworth Cengage Learning, 2011.

McWHIRTER, Robert J. *The First Amendment:* **An Illustrated History**. Tempe: Constitution Press, 2017.

MORONE, Piergiuseppe; PAPENDIEK, Franka; TARTIU, Valentina Elena. *Food Waste Reduction and Valorisation:* **Sustainability Assessment and Policy Analysis**. Cham: Springer International Publishing, 2017.

ROOSEVELT, Eleanor et al. *Universal Declaration of Human Rights*. Bedford: Applewood Books, 2001.

STROBEL, Tammy. *You Can Buy Happiness (and It's Cheap):* **How One Woman Radically Simplified Her Life and How You Can Too**. Novato: New World Library, 2012.

TAYLOR, Gabriela. *Advertising in a Digital Age:* **Best Practices & Tips for Paid Search and Social Media Advertising**. Bexhill-on-Sea: Global & Digital, 2013.

The Guardian, London, April 23, 2013.

The Guardian, London, October 13, 2016.

The Guardian, London, October 5, 2017.

The New York Times, New York, September 13, 2017.

The New York Times, New York, June 1, 2014.